FEED MY SHEEP

The Thought and Words of Philip Saliba

On the occasion of his twentieth year in the Episcopacy

edited by

JOSEPH J. ALLEN

ST VLADIMIR'S SEMINARY PRESS
CRESTWOOD, NEW YORK 10707
1987

Library of Congress Cataloging-in-Publication Data

Saliba, Philip, 1931-
Feed my sheep.

1. Antiochian Orthodox Christian Archdiocese
of North America—Miscellanea. 2. Orthodox
Eastern Church—Miscellanea. 3. Jewish-Arab
relations—1949-   —Miscellanea. 4. Lebanon—
History—1975-   —Miscellanea.   I. Allen,
Joseph J.   II. Title.
BX738.A5S24   1987   281.9   86-31579
ISBN 0-88141-066-7

FEED MY SHEEP

© Copyright 1987

by

ST VLADIMIR'S SEMINARY PRESS

ISBN 0-88141-066-7

PRINTED IN THE UNITED STATES OF AMERICA
BY
ATHENS PRINTING COMPANY
New York, NY 10018-6401

Contents

Introduction

It is, of course, impossible to capture in the words of a book all that a man is. But a man's own word sometimes gives us a glimpse of his inner life and vision; a word spoken—at least spoken sincerely—makes external that which is interior to his person. In the text which follows, one finds the words that reveal the person of Philip Saliba during his twenty years as an Orthodox bishop.

It is important to know this because this text is not a biography, nor a book about the particular programs and plans which have been realized during those years of his service; other works will show—and have shown—these particulars under Metropolitan Philip's extraordinary leadership. However, if one notes carefully these chosen words (which he has spoken and written over the years at various occasions and on various pertinent subjects), one will easily see what it is that underlies, i.e. what is at the root, and has motivated, those various programs associated with his name and ministry. In short, looking at the person, we can see the intent and aim that has given birth to such action.

Two important points must be made before the reader begins this book. The first point has to do with our grouping of the material. We have attempted to group into five distinct sections these "glimpses" into his person: Sanctification and Love, Ministry and Mission, Faith and Freedom, Orthodoxy and America, and The Old and New World. Indeed, one can tell immediately, by merely noting these chapter heads, that these words are at times personal and intimate; they take us to the inside of the person.

In conjunction with this, one should know that it was the

material itself which defined the categories; his thoughts and vision seemed to shape, almost naturally, our chapter titles. This is so because they mark the precise areas around which Philip has most often shown his concern. Our attempt has not been to give them in a chronological order, although we have presented the date and place of each thought or writing. Rather, at all times we have tried to use these categories to present the broadest picture of the man, i.e. to see where he has been, to understand his hope. This means, in turn, that we see him sometimes in his weakest moments, sometimes in his strength. As he was honest, so we are. Thus, for example, one sees in the material Philip's thoughts about the late Patriarch Elias IV of Antioch, whom he loved very much, thoughts about Father Alexander Schmemann with whom he had a long and special friendship, thoughts about Metropolitan Antony (Bashir), the well-known and admired predecessor whose shoes the young Philip—at the age of 35—was called to fill. One will also see this same honesty in the material regarding the broader areas of church and ministry. Again, we still see the person, but now as he reveals his vision regarding such issues as the Church in America, the various aspects of the Old World (of which sometimes he speaks with great joy, at other times with great frustration and disappointment), of the task of Orthodox clergy and their mission, of cultural concerns in the West, etc. One will especially see, when Philip speaks of his very early heart attack (and the spiritual trials surrounding it) a brutal honesty. At that time he reflects upon his fears, the moments of his utter despair and pride, and then, an impending and unfolding discernment of his own humanity—a true and natural humility in which he begins to discover that his only strength and hope is in God. In presenting the material, I have tried to hide none of it.

Thus, one will see in this material the true picture of the person of Philip Saliba, and his twenty years of ministry as Metropolitan of the Antiochian Orthodox Archdiocese of North America.

It should also be noted that the only material which has not been placed under these five groups are his Consecration

Speech, his Nativity Meditation of 1969, and his Paschal Meditation of 1971; these begin and end the text itself. The speech, delivered at St Elias Monastery in Dhour Shweir, Lebanon in 1966, remained without an acceptable translation (from the Arabic) until this publication. When it was originally published in the Middle East, i.e. in the various Arabic newspapers, it was hailed as a most unique "confession" of the young bishop. It stands *in toto* because, taken together, it also says much about the person, Philip Saliba. The other piece is Philip's Paschal Meditation of 1971, in which the Metropolitan sees, amidst his busy "American" schedule as a bishop, the central point—the nexus—of all that activity: the Agony, Crucifixion and Resurrection of Our Lord Jesus Christ. It also stands as a fine expression of the man.

Besides the categories, the second important point has to do with the title of the book, *Feed My Sheep*. It is taken from the post-resurrection narrative of the Gospel of John (21:15-19) between Our Lord Jesus Christ and Peter. The question "Do you Love me?" is asked three times by Jesus. Each time Peter responds: "Lord, you know I do," and after each of Peter's responses, Our Lord concludes "Feed My Sheep." These two, loving Christ and feeding the sheep, are the two poles of ministry for any true Christian disciple of the Lord and His Church. It is in the space between these two poles where the ministry of Christ is to be lived and practiced. However, not withstanding the fact that this challenging—and yet most tender—dialogue lends itself to various and important points of exegesis (e.g. in the language used, or in Peter's seeming frustration with Christ's insistent question), this same dialogue most simply and fundamentally offers itself as a title of the book for obvious reasons. Allow me an explanation.

This writer, perhaps more than any other (and due to certain natural reasons), has been at many ordinations celebrated by Metropolitan Philip. It is from this scriptural pericope (Jn 21:15-19) that he most often preaches at those times. Judging from the content of his proclamation, he uses this dialogue because he seems to have sensed that any person who will serve in this ministry of the disciple must, in fact and indeed, enter—and struggle *to remain*—in this space between loving Christ and feeding His sheep. Who can serve a ministry (whether clergy or laity) without loving Christ? And who can truly love Christ without seeing that that love is manifested in a ministry (service), i.e. in feeding His sheep? In short, what is ministry if not feeding the flock because we love Christ? This is the space in which the disciple must live, and each of these times when he has preached, Philip has invited the person being ordained into that space. There is no better title by which to label Metropolitan Philip's thoughts and words.

Finally, a personal note. After having thoroughly searched all his talks and writings during this past year (1986), Philip's twentieth year as Metropolitan and Archbishop, it has been my particular joy and honor to have had a small part in presenting this glimpse into his person. As we now present these thoughts and words, we likewise invite the reader into the mind and heart of the man.

Joseph Allen
August 14, 1986

Nativity Meditation 1969

by METROPOLITAN PHILIP

Lord,
What shall I offer you at your Nativity in return for your
infinite love?
I have neither gold nor silver, neither myrrh nor frankincense.
My house is without a roof. I have no room for you, not
even a manger.
My soul is even darker than the clouds of my passion.
My eyes are too dim to look beyond the horizon of myself.
Help me behold your bright star; "For in thy light shall we
see light."

Lord,
You have been knocking on my door for many years,
but I never dared let you in because my garment is not white
as snow.
Forgive me if I do not invite you to my table,
for my table is full of everything you despise.
I have betrayed you more than Judas.
I have denied you more than Peter
I have doubted you more than Thomas.
My hands are empty. My lips are not clean to sing your praise.
And my heart is wrinkled with sorrow like a withered leaf
under
autumn's wind.

Lord,

The only thing I can offer you at your Nativity is myself.
Drown me in the ocean of your love.
Feed me with your heavenly bread, for the bread of this
world will never satisfy my hunger.
Quench my thirst with your divine fountain, for the water of
this earth will never satisfy my thirst.
Give me your eyes to see what you see, your ears to hear
what you hear and your heart to love what you love.
Take me with you to Mount Tabor and let me bathe in your
eternal light.
"Create a clean heart in me. Cast me not away from Thy face.
Restore unto me the joy of Thy salvation, and strengthen me
with a perfect spirit."
Teach me how to pray in simple words, for only through
    prayers
may I overcome my loneliness.
Help me to care for the needy, the oppressed, the orphans,
the sinners and the despised whom you love.
As I kneel before your manger with love and humility
I beseech you to listen to my prayers.

I

On Sanctification and Love

"Whosoever believes that Jesus is the Christ, is born of God: and everyone that loves Him who has created life, loves those who were created by Him."

(I John 5:1)

"For both He who sanctifies, and they that are sanctified are all one: for which cause He is not ashamed to call them brethern."

(Hebrews 2:11)

After Liturgy on the Eve of the Nativity I am alone but not lonely, because in Christ Jesus there is no loneliness and there is no separation. The walls are destroyed and the barriers are no more. The Child of the manger has reconciled everything to Himself; henceforth, there is no race, no color, no conflict and no hatred; in Him there is "a new heaven and a new earth." St Isaac the Syrian said:

What is a merciful heart? It is a heart that burns with love for the whole creation—for men, for birds, for beasts, for demons and for every creature.

Christmas Eve, 1982

Christmas Eve, to me, is a time for reflection. The year is slowly sinking into the ocean of eternity, and in my reflection, there are painful questions:

Did I love Him enough? Did I serve Him enough? Did I suffer enough? Did I forgive enough? How many tears did I dry? How many wounds did I bind? Was I faithful to Him who loved me beyond measure?

How loving and compassionate is God that despite my sinfulness and unworthiness He "became flesh and dwelt amongst us." What an unfathomable condescension that He assumed our nature in order to make us "partakers" of His nature.

Christmas Eve, 1982

The first time I walked on the beach after my heart operation I felt like kissing every grain of sand, hugging every wave and embracing the whole world. A few days before Thanksgiving I returned home and went straight to the altar of St John's Chapel and prayed from the depth of my heart. The trees around the house were naked, the leaves were wrinkled and the flowers were dead. Thus with much lust for life I began to dream, with the naked trees, the wrinkled leaves and the dead flowers of another spring, another youth conference and another summer.

"Personal Reflections:
from heart attack to heart surgery," 1972

The towers which man has built ended in utter confusion, despair and destruction. Despite the painful lessons of history, we continue to build towers and turn our eyes away from the splendid glory of God. As a result of all this, we find ourselves, as T.S. Eliot said, in a "wasteland," in a spiritual vacuum. We have too much to live on, but nothing to live for. IF bread alone is sufficient, why then all our frustration, anxiety, fear, boredom and despair?

Pittsburgh, 1970

The doctrine of man in our theology is based on the biblical view which was fully defined by our Church Fathers. Man has all the potentialities for perfection, simply because he was created in the image of God. St Maximus the Confessor states:

Those who have followed Christ in action and contemplation, will be changed into an even better condition, and there is no time to tell all the ascents and revelations of the saints who are being changed from glory to glory, until each one in order receives deification.

Man was not created to be a slave, neither to society nor to history, neither to science nor to technology, neither to communism nor to capitalism. Even though nature has limitations, these limitations can be overcome by the sacramental life of the Church.

Pittsburgh, 1970

In order to solve the difficult problems which have been facing us, we must concentrate first and above all on the human personality, which has been distorted by hate and sin. Instead of directing our efforts to demonstrations, civil disobedience and other violent and negative actions, we must try to rid the American society of its inherited complexes of hate, fear and prejudice.

"Christ, Social Justice and Violence," 1979

Many civil rights leaders could be murdered, but their blood throughout this land will continue to cry "murderers, assassins, and slaves to your hate and fear!" Many American cities could be burned by the fires of chaos and destruction but we profit nothing. Unless we burn by the holy fire the hate and the slavery from the American heart, neither the Black nor the White will find peace, freedom or justice in this land.

"Christ, Social Justice and Violence," 1979

Therefore, our revolution must begin in the heart of the individual citizen. Harmony and peace in this land must be the reflection of our inner peace and serenity. Unless this inner tranquility is achieved on a personal basis, the might, the wealth, and all the glory of this nation will be reduced to ashes. Violence breeds violence, hatred breeds hatred and chaos breed chaos. Ultimately, unless the divine image is restored to the American personality, we will legislate in vain, labour in vain and hope in vain.

"Christ, Social Justice and Violence," 1979

St Basil spoke against such an unchristian attitude and lack of love:

Woe unto them that join house to house 'til there be no place for others. (Is 5:8) And what do you do? Do you not find a thousand pretexts to rob your neighbor? You say, his house stands in my light; it is too noisy; tramps go there. On one pretext or another you drive him out, persecute him 'til you force him to move. The sea knows its boundaries; the night does not overstep its appointed limits. But a possessive man has no respect for time, does not recognize boundaries; like fire, he attacks everything and swallows it up.

(Homily Against the Rich)

Indeed, the Church Fathers were very mindful and fundamentally opposed to social evils.

"Christ, Social Justice and Violence," 1979

Christ and His Church did not compromise with social evils and social injustice, yet they were fundamentally against reducing the eternal message of the Gospel into nothing but social action. The militant Church is struggling in the world, yet she is not of this world. A good Christian must never forget that heaven is his ultimate goal and that he has no permanent city here on earth. "Seek ye first the Kingdom of God and His righteousness; and all these things shall be added unto you." (Matt 7:33)

"Christ, Social Justice and Violence," 1979

Nikos Kazantzakis in his book *The Saviours of God* said, "we are living in a critical, violent moment of history. An entire world is crashing down. Our epoch is not a moment of equilibrium in which refinement, reconciliation, peace, and love might be fruitful virtues." Dissatisfaction marks our age and disturbs our happiness. We have become detached from ourselves, from others, from nature, and ultimately from God. We are, as Camus said, "strangers" in the world. Our society is stricken by mental disorders, violence and crimes. We have lost our sense of destiny. We are nobody, from nowhere, going no place. Alienation is the stigma of our age. This word "alienation" has been used by philosophers, psychologists and sociologists to refer to an extra-ordinary variety of psycho-social disorders including self-anxiety, despair, ruthlessness, apathy, social disorganization, loneliness, meaninglessness, isolation, pessimism and the loss of beliefs or values.

"Reflections," 1981

To glorify Jesus Christ through a life of service and witness is to love people, and experience within our congregations a genuine Christian *Koinonia.*

To the Clergy, 1980

Whenever we glance through the pages of the Old Testament, we come across women who by their love have served the Divine purpose by their examples, their life and good deeds; such as Sarah, who was called the "Mother of Nations," such as Rebecca, Rachel, and Ruth.

"On Women and Christianity," 1983

We also read in the New Testament that many women followed Jesus, some of them were more faithful to Him than His own disciples. Remember that Peter denied Him, Judas betrayed Him, and Thomas doubted Him. And during the darkest hour of His agony on the cross, all His disciples deserted Him except John, and a few women who were there at Calvary watching Him with torn hearts.

"On Women and Christianity," 1983

First and foremost, I am a pastor; this is how I lived as a priest and continue to live as a shepherd to my flock. My main concern for the past twenty-five years has been to find meaning in people; not in words, concepts or abstract theological speculation. If we can define theology as "the study of God and His relation to the world"; if we can say, "the Word became flesh" (John 1:14); if we can say, "for God so loved the world" (John 3:16); if we can say that God became man in order to make us "partakers of the Divine Nature" (II Peter 1:4); and if we can say that the purpose of the incarnation was to redeem man and the entire cosmos, we can then rightly say that any theology which does not touch man in his joy and sorrow, his hope and despair, his faith and doubt, his sickness and health, his poverty and wealth, and his life and death, is abstract and meaningless theology.

Commencement Address,
St Vladimir's Seminary, 1981

I have never known a priest to fail because he did not know theology, but I have known several priests who failed because they could not communicate with people. If you know everything about horses and do not know how to ride a horse, what is the use of your knowledge? By the same token, if you know everything about God, but fail to make Him alive in the hearts of your people, what is the use of your theology?

Commencement Address,
St Vladimir's Seminary, 1981

Four priests gathered together to discuss the various translations of the Bible. The first one said, "I like the King James translation because of its beauty." The second one said, "I like the Douhay translation because it is accurate." The third one said, "I like the revised translation because it is simple." The fourth one said, "I like my mother's translation." The rest of the priests asked him, "We didn't know your mother translated the Bible?" He said "Yes, she did. She translated the Bible into life." Motherhood sanctifies our lives.

"Women and Christianity," 1983

In the book of Genesis, we read the following: "Then God said, 'Let us make man in our image, after our likeness . . .'" (Gen 1:26). This does not apply only to the white man, but to all men regardless of color, race, or creed. God has blessed all of life, giving His image to all human beings.

"Christ, Social Justice and Violence," 1979

The Russian author, Evgeny Barabanov in a recent essay entitled "Schism Between Church and the World" said: "It is impossible for man to settle in the world completely without God. Although proud of its successes and attainments, the world sees every day more clearly the provisional and insufficient nature of its civilization. On the verge of having its foundations shaken to the core, it thirsts as never before for the true light." Unfortunately, only a few prophets such as Barabanov and Solzhenitsyn understand the tragedy of man under both capitalism and communism. We read in the Psalms that God made man "a little lower than the angels and has crowned him with glory and honor" (Psalm 8:5). Yet our economic systems, philosophical concepts and modern technology has dehumanized man and reduced him to an object of psychological and natural categories.

"On Contemporary Iconoclasm," Pittsburgh, 1976.

In her book *Scenes of Clerical Life*, George Eliot wrote, "Ideas are often poor ghosts . . . but sometimes they are made flesh; they breathe upon us with warm breath; they touch as with soft responsive hands . . . and speak to us in appealing tones; they are clothed in a living, human soul, with all its conflicts, its faith, and its love. Then their presence is a power, then they shake us like a passion." If you do not experience love and compassion in a personal way, do not preach about love; you cannot fool the people. We are more transparent than we think.

Commencement Address,
St Vladimir's Seminary, 1981

We must be fully aware that our Church and our entire world are faced with the most serious and most dangerous problems in history. Let us migrate from the world for a while to our inner selves and examine whether my statement means anything. Self-awareness means full cognizance of our place in this world *vis-a-vis* God, man and nature. According to the biblical view, man was created in the "image of God and His likeness." The poet David, in Psalm 8, tells us that man was made "little less than God." He was crowned with honor and glory and all things were put under his feet. By his own actions and free will, man refused that divine freedom, thus alienating himself from God, his fellow man and nature.

Pittsburgh, 1970

If one reads the Scripture, he will find that all those who have had a profound encounter with God became radically changed. We may know the human only when we are confronted by the divine, we may know the temporal only when we ponder the eternal, and we may know the peak of the mountain only when we look at it from the depths of the valley. We are sick and paralyzed by fear and will never be healed without a true encounter with Christ.

Pittsburgh, 1970

You cannot give yourself in love and you cannot empty yourself, unless you find that self through meditation and prayer.

Commencement Address,
St Vladimir's Seminary, 1981

"For I will restore health to you,
and your wounds I will heal."

(Jer 30:17)

Between May and September of 1972 the pain in my chest had increased and I became convinced that I must undergo open heart surgery. After intense consultation with some of the great doctors throughout the country, I decided that the Miami Heart Institute was the place which may satisfy the cry of my heart for more blood.

It has been my practice that before I make a long trip, I usually answer all my mail and leave my office in good order. Wednesday, September 13, everything was ready; my desk was clear, my suitcase was packed and a room was reserved at the hospital for this major surgery. A short conference was held with my office personnel and it was time for departure. The old and majestic oak trees which lovingly and watchfully surround my home were still green and as beautiful as ever. The last thing I did before I left home was my visit with God at St John Chrysostom's Chapel. If there are "pieces of heaven" on earth, the chapel of St John is one of them. As I was leaving the Chapel, my eyes caught a glimpse of the words inscribed above its door, "Dedicated to Teen SOYO. June 3, 1972." I thought of our little children, the Teen SOYO, the youth, our Archdiocese, and all the beautiful things that we can live for, then suddenly a feeling of indescribable joy permeated my soul and as I left home I was certain more than ever that I would be coming back to continue God's work with a healthier heart and much hope for a very promising future for our youth and our Church in the New World.

"Personal Reflections:
from heart attack to heart surgery," 1972

This psychological change from hopelessness to hopefulness was the greatest thing which happened to me in the hospital. The state of despair which encompassed my soul as a result of the heart attack in 1968 resulted from personal pride and some misunderstanding of the problem of suffering. I refused to accept the reality of my illness because I was young, strong, proud of my youth, and wherever I traveled I often heard, "Isn't he young? Isn't he strong? Isn't he dynamic?" I really believed that I was young, strong and immune from all illness. I also believed that I could change history. I had my plans for the Archdiocese, for Orthodoxy in America, for the Mother Church, for the Arab Refugees and for the complicated political situation in the Middle East. In other words I was trying to build my own Babylonian Tower and not the Kingdom of God. Wasn't the sin of pride the cause of our alienation from God? After this leap into the darkness I began to see the light. I began to identify my suffering with the Cross. I began to feel that I was united with all those who suffer on this earth. "For if one member suffers all suffer together" (I Cor 12:26). Moreover, I began to understand Christ's compassion for the sick, the blind, the paralyzed, the widow who lost her only son, the sinful woman and all sinners. Suffering can be extremely destructive if it is not understood in the light of the empty tomb. Goethe once said: "He who does not eat his bread with sorrow, he who does not spend the midnight hours weeping and waiting for the dawn, does not know you, ye heavenly powers." Through creative suffering I completely surrendered my life to God. Without faith in Him and without His sustaining power, we are nothing but "dust and ashes." "Even though I walk through the valley of the shadow of death, I fear no evil; for thou art with me; thy rod and thy staff, they comfort me" (Psalm 23:4). Surrendering to God made me feel, for the first time, at peace with myself, with others and with the world. "Henceforth," I said to God, "my life belongs to you. You can do with it whatever you want. If you feel that my life has a purpose in your world, then let me become an instrument of your Divine plan, and if you feel otherwise, let me fade away in the darkness of the grave; for a little flower in your field still has its fragrance and beauty...."

"From Pride, to Suffering, to Hope:
from heart attack to heart surgery," 1972

In the second Epistle of St Peter it is said: "His Divine power has granted to us all things that pertain to life and godliness, through the knowledge of Him who called us to

His own glory and excellence, by which He has granted to us His precious and very great promises, that through these you may escape from the corruption that is in the world because of passion, and become partakers of the divine nature" (II Peter 1:3-5). The whole aim of the Christian life is "theosis" or deification. It is that ultimate union and free communion with God. St Irenaeus said: "The Word of God, Jesus Christ, on account of His great love for mankind, became what we are in order to make us what He, Himself, is." He humanized His nature in order to divinize ours.

Charleston, 1976

If your personality is disintegrated and the image of God in you is distorted, then your actions will undoubtedly reflect that disintegration and distortion.

Pittsburgh, 1970

Each and every one of us can become Christ-like through prayer, contemplation and action. St Maximus further says:

While remaining in his soul and body entirely man by nature, he becomes in his soul and body entirely God by grace. Deification involves the whole human being.

All the ancient Greek dichotomy between body and soul disappears in St Maximus. When God created man, he created him as a whole being: and when man collapsed, he collapsed not partially but as a whole being, and when man was redeemed, he was redeemed totally, body and soul. Through the sacrament of the Holy Eucharist God enters into union with the whole man.

"Personal Reflections," 1972

The Incarnation has a cosmic dimension, but the primary purpose of God's marvelous and decisive intervention in human history was to embrace man and restore to him that divine sonship and that divine image which was distorted by sin. "When the fullness of the time was come, God sent forth His son, made of a woman, made under the law to redeem them that were under the law, that we might receive the adoption of sons" (Gal 4:4-6).

"On Contemporary Iconoclasm,"
Pittsburgh, 1976

My beloved friends, let me remind you again that the gate is narrow and the road is difficult, and unless we become serious about this glorious faith it will be taken away from us. If we want to ascend to the peak of the mountain and bathe with the eternal light of the Transfiguration, we have to make a painful decision and commit ourselves totally to the agony of the Cross. Nicholas Berdyaev said: "No man who is divided can be free, and a man who cannot make the free act of choosing the object of his love, is condemned to this division."

Can you then drink His Cup? Can you accept His Baptism of Fire? Are you willing to go through Hell in order to reach the Gates of Paradise? If you are willing to do so, you will reach the peak, you will destroy all boundaries, you will overcome all limitation, and finally, you will gloriously shout with Nikos Kazantzakis: "Die every moment, but say, 'Death does not exist.'"

Miami, 1969

The past is history. History becomes meaningful when time is dedicated to the fulfillment of God's purpose in it. In his book *The Meaning of History*, Nicholas Berdyaev said: "History is a process, movement and fulfillment within time. The significance we attach to history is directly determined by that which we attribute to time."

Only in this light we can look at the past and examine seriously whether our actions have sanctified time or made of it nothing but a profanity.

Boston, 1971

What better goals can we strive for than those goals already set for us by our Lord and Master Himself? "Seek ye first the Kingdom of God and His righteousness and everything else will be added unto you." When a man came to Jesus asking Him, "What shall I do to inherit eternal life?" Our Lord answered in simple words, "Thou shalt love the Lord thy God with all your heart, with all your mind, with all your soul and your neighbor as yourself."

These goals are not easy to attain by any means. For to seek the Kingdom of God in the midst of all these worldly and demonic kingdoms, is very difficult, and to love God and neighbor in a world so indifferent to God and neighbor, is most difficult indeed. We may reach the farthest planet in this cosmos, but if we don't have love, we are nothing. Author Emmet Fox wrote, "There is no difficulty that enough love will not conquer, no disease that enough love will not heal, no door that enough love will not open, no gulf that enough love will not bridge, no wall that enough love will not throw down, no sin that enough love will not redeem. If only you could love enough, you would be the happiest and most powerful being in the world."

Los Angeles, 1972

It was such a beautiful experience to see parents and children praying and playing together in a true spirit of Christian fellowship . . . We now have a thousand years of spirituality and family traditions to sustain us. Man is not an object to be enslaved and abused by political systems and de-humanized by strange intellectual trends. Man is a child of God and an heir of His Kingdom, and according to our theology, he is a partaker of the Divine nature. We must, therefore, concentrate on the spiritual renewal of the individual if we want to live in a peaceful world.

Montreal, 1974

Despite these cries and despite our human frailty and blindness, the Light, which darkness cannot overcome, continues to shine. Human history is a combination of bright and dark moments. May God grant us wisdom to interpret historical events in a prophetic way and may we also understand that the dark moments of history are the work of the devil who despises light. I am sure that all of us, at one time or another, have experienced within ourselves this tremendous tension between light and darkness. St Simeon the New Theologian wrote:

I have often seen the light. Sometimes it has appeared to me within myself, when my soul possessed peace and silence. Sometimes it has appeared only at a distance, and at times it was even hidden completely. Then I experienced great affliction believing that I will never see it again. But from the moment when I began to shed tears, when I bore witness to a complete detachment from everything and to an absolute humility and obedience, the light appeared once again like the sun which penetrates the thickness of the clouds.

Thus, to be immersed in the light of the empty tomb and to bathe in the light of the Transfiguration, one has to weep and detach himself from self-centeredness, arrogance and pride. Have we witnessed to this Light in faith and in deeds?

Montreal, 1974

The sacraments become means of grace and life only through the work of the Holy Spirit; otherwise, they are nothing but empty rituals.

Louisville, 1975

Last October, on the eve of the dedication of the Antiochian Village, we celebrated an open air Vesper Service on that beautiful mountain. While the choir was chanting, "O Gladsome Light," the bright sun was slowly sinking beyond the horizon, half covered by the yellow leaves of the Pennsylvania trees. I felt like bending down and kissing the ground because the place was holy. I saw God face to face in His eternal glory. I saw Him in every individual who prayed with me on the mountain. We have spent enough time, energy and money chasing planes from one hotel to another, and we have spent more than enough time talking and hearing about God. I am tired of that. My young people, I am sure, are also tired of hearing about God. There is a deafening noise in the media about God, yet nobody sees Him. We no longer want to hear about Jesus of Nazareth. We want to meet Him, face to face, and talk to Him.

Miami, 1979

Little children are little poets. They are full of wonder and amazement. I wish we could see the world the way children see it and celebrate life the way children celebrate it. The most sincere love is the love of children and the most genuine innocence is the innocence of children. Our Lord said: "Except ye be converted, and become as little children, ye shall not enter the kingdom of heaven" (Matt 18:2-4). Only if you are child-like, may you enter the kingdom of heaven. God's kingdom will have more "children" than bishops, priests, philosophers, politicians, and so-called leaders of this world.

Miami, 1979

Despite the fact that I left home when I was young, I still remember my childhood very vividly. My parents did not have much material wealth but they had much love. The few things which we had we shared, and that was the secret of our happiness. The report of the Carnegie Council on children states: "Where poverty is shared, in the security of a stable family and a functioning cultural environment, a child would not suffer."

Miami, 1979

Dear Stephanie,

Like the twinkling of an eye, the years will swiftly pass and you will be able to read this love letter. I loved you, Stephanie, when I married your Mom and Dad in our little chapel. I loved you even more on the day of your baptism when you were born of "water and spirit."

"Letter to the Child, Stephanie," 1986

Some day, if I am around, I will remind you of the day when we had lunch together. It was one of the happiest days of my life. Although I do not speak your language and you cannot speak mine, we had no problem communicating. Love, my dear little Stephanie, transcends all languages and overcomes all barriers. The gestures of your little hands were like the fluttering of a bird's wings and your angelic smile was as beautiful as God's smile when He created the world and "everything was good." When I look at your face, Stephanie, I remember the moments when the world was pure and innocent. It is a pity that we have to grow old and lose that innocence.

"Letter to the Child, Stephanie," 1986

In order for children to grow up well adjusted to life, they need more than money, bread and meat; they need love. There was a time when we did not have much money, much bread and much meat and yet, we were happy. Today, we have all these things and yet, we are unhappy. When Christ said: "Man shall not live by bread alone," He expressed the eternal truth. It is indeed unfortunate that millions of children are being raised by Day Care Centers in this country and by the State in Communist countries. How can a child experience his parent's love if he is raised by faceless people? Mueller Fahrenhold said:

What a child has learned, no one can take away again, and this applies to suffering as well as to happiness.

Miami, 1979

Traveling in this Archdiocese during the past thirteen years, I have had the most wonderful encounters with our little children. They call me all kinds of names, e.g., some call me "Your Innocence," some "Your M & M, some "St Edna," and some believe that I am the "Imperial Margarine King." Children are the most precious gifts which we receive from God. I have a special file in my office which contains the most beautiful letters from children.

Miami, 1979

Our study of history and the events which are shaping our world today, prove beyond doubt, that without Christ this world will continue to be hopeless and aimless and our lives will continue to be subjected to decadence, corruption and death. St Paul said: "If anyone is in Christ, he is a new creation, the old has passed away, behold the new has come" (II Cor 5:17). Only God's love which we experience in Christ can transform our inner beings and create new hearts within us, give us new minds, renew our families, transfigure our parishes, and ultimately transform the entire world. All these things can happen to us, "if we do not accept the grace of God in vain."

Miami, 1981

Last, but not least, Your Beatitude, I want to say a few words about our little children. The children of our Archdiocese are the real source of my inspiration. They never cease to amaze me with their curiosity, humor, innocence and genuine love. After the June War of 1967, I was raising funds for the Palestinian refugees in Allentown, Pennsylvania. When I finished my sermon on the plight of the refugees, an eight-year-old altar boy reached into his pocket and handed me a quarter. I am sure that quarter was all that he had. Five years ago, during the dark days of the Lebanese War, after preaching about the agony of the Lebanese children, a little girl in Boston, took off her ring and gave it to me saying, "this is for the Lebanese children."

"Addressing Patriarch Ignatius," Boston, 1985

II

On Ministry and Mission

"Not that we are sufficient of ourselves, to think anything as of ourselves. But our sufficiency is of God; who also has made us able ministers of the new testament. . . . Therefore, seeing we have this ministry, as we have received mercy, we faint not. . . . For we preach not ourselves, but Christ Jesus the Lord; and ourselves your servants for Jesus' sake."

(II Cor 3:5,6; 4:1,5)

Why this sudden emphasis on Mission? Is this some kind of innovation or a new fad in the life of the Church? The answer is in the Scripture which is our most authentic and authoritative point of reference. From reading the Gospels, we learn that our Lord was the perfect missionary. Was He not sent to us by the Father on a redemptive mission and did His earthly ministry not clearly reflect this reality? In the New Testament, we read: "He went about all Galilee, teaching in the synagogues and preaching the gospel of the Kingdom and healing every disease and every infirmity among the people" (Matt 4:23).

Charleston, 1978

Metropolitan Antony did not leave any files to speak of, because his mind was his file and he grew up with the Archdiocese. Our financial system and our annual budget were too inadequate to answer the future needs of the Archdiocese. Some of our priests were neither liturgically nor psychologically fit to serve an Eastern Orthodox Church. There was an awesome task ahead of me and the difficult thing was where to begin. My main concern was to know my flock and my clergy first. Thus I embarked on a visitation program which took me to almost every parish within the Archdiocese. I found our people warm, hospitable, receptive to new ideas and very eager to join hands with me to work for a brighter future of our Church on this continent.

"The Year of Difficulties and Loneliness," 1970

I asked one of my priests once: "Father, why don't you go after these seventy-five families and bring them back to Christ?" He said: "Saidna, they are no good." I said: "This is precisely why you should minister to them. If they are no good, it is our duty to make them good. Our Lord said: 'Those who are well have no need of a physician, but those who are sick; I came not to call the righteous but sinners'" (Mark 2:17).

Charleston, 1978

The heart—and the pain—of mission is found in the story of the seventeenth chapter of the Book of Acts:

Paul and Silas went to Thessalonica to preach the gospel. Many Greeks, men and women, embraced the new faith. But the Jews were jealous, and taking some wicked fellows of the rabble, they gathered a crowd, set the city in an uproar, and attacked the house of Jason, seeking to bring them out to the people. And when they could not find them, they dragged Jason and some of the brethren before the city authorities crying, "These men who have turned the world upside down have come here also. (Acts 17:5-6).

Are we not also called to "turn the world upside down"?

Charleston, 1978

I once heard a story about a man who was on a horse galloping swiftly along the road. An old farmer, standing in the fields, seeing him pass by, called out: "Hey, rider, where are you going?" The rider turned around and shouted back, "Don't ask me, ask the horse."

We lose our identity as shepherds, as servants of our people, when we fail to know where our horses are going.

When we feel that we are losing our direction, I believe that it is spiritually refreshing to take refuge in the Scripture and the writings of the Fathers.

"To the Clergy," 1978

Every sermon has meaning and value only when it is the result of personal spiritual experience and knowledge. Every sermon pronounced only with our lips is dead and false and those who listen always unmistakably feel it.

"To the Clergy," 1978

In the Book of Acts 1:8, Christ told His disciples, "But you shall receive power when the Holy Spirit has come upon you; and you shall be my witnesses in Jerusalem and in all Judea and Samaria and to the end of the earth." Our Lord commanded His disciples to be witnesses after they received "power from on high." Thus the missionary spirit in the Church is deeply rooted in the eternal Christian message; the Church was born as a missionary movement which changed history.

Charleston, 1978

Orthodoxy, despite her past glory, remains the best kept secret in this land because of our failure to understand the missionary dimensions of the Church. America does not understand us because we are still talking to her in languages which she does not understand. We are still talking to America as Greeks, Russians, Serbians, Ukrainians, Romanians, etc. No wonder, then, that six millon Orthodox have no presence on the American scene.

"Anticipating: On the Future of the Church in America," 1977

Remember, you are not in the parish to dominate but to serve, to discover and cultivate talent. If the priest really wants to be an agent of spiritual change, the first thing he has to learn is how to *share* leadership. It is amazing to find that most priests are still working very much on their own and have not yet found the creative ways to mobilize the potential leadership in their parishes and share their responsibilities with others. Congregations can be transformed only when priests and laymen come together in a spirit of charity and humility.

Commencement Address,
St Vladimir's Seminary, 1981

Some of our priests go to a parish expecting to make it a song of praise to the Almighty God in one month or in one year. Thus if their efforts do not bring forth concrete and immediate results, they become disappointed, bitter, angry or indifferent. We often forget that God does not make things happen according to our calendar. He makes things happen in His own way and in His own time. After all, He did not call you to succeed in restructuring the whole world, but to structure your priorities and remain faithful to His word.

Commencement Address,
St Vladimir's Seminary, 1981

With the priest, there is a great temptation of pride. Some of those who want to change society are in danger of putting themselves over it and being more conscious of the weaknesses of others than of the weakness of their own soul. Very often we are very busy going from meeting to meeting and from function to function. We want to be everywhere and yet we are afraid to enter the sanctuary of our soul, to be alone and face the fact that we are in just as much need of change as the congregation we are trying to convert.

Commencement Address,
St Vladimir's Seminary, 1981

St John Chrysostom and St Basil the Great were among the most outspoken Fathers against social injustice and the monopoly of wealth. "Say not I am spending what is my own, I am enjoying what is my own. No, not your own, but other people's. Precisely because you make an inhuman use of it and say 'I have a right for my personal enjoyment that which belongs to me,' I maintain that those possessions do not belong to you. They belong together to you and your neighbors, just as sunshine, air, earth and all the rest." (Chrysostom, *Homily 10 on Corinthians I*) "Who is covetous? He who is not content with what is sufficient. Who is a robber? He who takes away other people's property. Are you not covetous? Are you not a robber if you make your own that which has been given you in stewardship? He who takes another's clothing is called a thief, he who does not clothe the naked, although he could do so, deserves no better name. The corn which you store belongs to the hungry; the cloak which you keep in your trunk belongs to the naked; the shoes which are rotting in your house belong to those who go barefoot; the silver which you hid in the ground belongs to the needy." (St Basil, *Homily 6:7*) These great Fathers are speaking to us today.

"Christ, Social Justice and Violence," 1979

The diaconate in the early Church was established for a social purpose:

Therefore, brethren, pick out from among you seven

men of good repute, full of the spirit and of wisdom, whom we may appoint to this duty" (Acts 6:5).

The main responsibility of the deacons was to distribute the offerings of the faithful to the poor.

In the *Didache* (an early Christian document) we read the following:

Thou must not refuse the need but share everything with thy brethren. Say not that this is thy property, for if we enjoy together the eternal blessings, it should be the more so with temporal ones.

Is this not a lesson to all of us, clergy and laity?

"Christ, Social Justice and Violence," 1979

In the Epistle to the Hebrews it is said: "Let us be concerned for one another, to help one another, to show love and to do good. Let us not give up the habit of meeting together as some are doing" (Chapter 10:24-25). The Book of Acts and the primitive Christian writings tell us that the early Christians came together for three main reasons:

1. To worship the Triune God and celebrate the Eucharist

2. To preach the Good News and experience a genuine Christian *Koinonia*

3. To glorify Jesus Christ through a life of witness and service.

I believe that these principles were true yesterday, are true today and will always be true until the end of history.

"To the Clergy," 1980

The Church started as a worshiping community. Even during the era of persecution, the Church never failed to come together for worship and the celebration of the Eucharist. Notice that I did not use the term "to perform the Divine Liturgy," because the early Christians did not "act" the liturgy; they celebrated it. To celebrate an event is to observe it in a very special way. The priests and the congregation are the celebrators while Christ is the celebrity *par excellence*. To celebrate the Eucharist is to encounter Christ in His manger, in His public ministry, in His suffering, death and resurrection from the dead. No other Christian can celebrate these special and unique events in human history the way the Orthodox Church does.

"To the Clergy," 1980

Twenty years from now our Church will enter the Twenty-first century. What our future Church will be depends on what you are today. I have tried to serve you to the best of my ability and if I have stumbled along the way, it is because of human frailty. Do not forget, however, that I love you and care for each and every one of you.

"To the Clergy," 1980

The vocation to which you have been called is most challenging if you take it seriously. You cannot face the challenge of your calling if you do not continue to grow spiritually. St John Chrysostom likened life to a battle. Listen to him speak:

You stand always in the front rank of battle, and are always receiving new wounds, . . . now your wife irritates you, then your son worries you, an enemy sets his snare for you, a friend speaks badly of you, a neighbor abuses you, a colleague deceives you, poverty oppresses you, the loss of those related to you afflicts you, fortune makes you arrogant, and misfortune makes you downcast. All around us are numerous opportunities for inducing in us anger, worry, discouragement, affliction, vanity and despair. Therefore, we need the divine medicine by which we may heal the wounds we have received.

"To the Clergy," 1980

What an eloquent description of the human condition. This is pastoral theology.

During the apostolic and patristic eras many women ministered to the sick, the orphans, and the needy ones. Special orders for women were established by the Church, such as the deaconess to help in the work of charity and social relief.

"On Women and Christianity," 1983

Those who are not familiar with the Orthodox Church think that we are just a ceremonial church. This is very far from the truth. Preaching has always been an essential part of the eucharistic celebration. Otherwise, why the Liturgy of the Word? During the eucharistic celebration, two kinds of communion take place: communion with the Word and communion with the Body and Blood of Christ. St Paul said: "Woe unto me if I do not preach the Gospel" (1 Cor. 9:16).

"To the Clergy," 1980

St John Chrysostom said:

We, to whom the ministry of the Word is entrusted, have received from the dear God the command never to abandon our duty and never to be silent, whether anyone listens to us or not. There are those priests who make fun of us and say, 'stop the good advice, scrap the admonitions, they will not listen to you, let them go.' What are you saying? Have you promised to convert all men in one day? If only ten, or only five, or indeed only one repents, is not that consolation enough?

I say: Be always prepared and ready to preach regardless of the size of your congregation.

"To the Clergy," 1980

Always remember that you are not "one of the boys," that is, you are not the insurance man, you are not the plumber, you are not the undertaker—you are the priest. You have been sent to save souls and not to be stumbling blocks.

"To the Clergy," 1978

A priest is a soldier in the army of Christ and he is expected to fight on the front to which he is assigned. Disobedience does not benefit anyone. Moreover, the priest who disobeys his bishop loses the respect, not only of his bishop, but of his community and ultimately he brings disaster upon himself.

"To the Clergy," 1978

The proclamation of the Gospel is the heart of the Liturgy of the Word. In his second Epistle to Timothy, St Paul said: "I charge you in the presence of God and of Christ Jesus who is to judge the living and the dead, and by His appearing, and His kingdom: preach the word, be urgent in season and out of season. Convince, rebuke, and exhort, be unfailing in patience and in teaching." (4:1-3) Again in First Corinthians, St Paul said: "Woe unto me if I do not preach the Gospel." (9:6) In Matthew, Our Lord admonishes us to "Go and make disciples of all nations." (28:19) How can we make disciples of all nations if we do not preach the "good news?"

Commencement Address,
St Vladimir's Seminary, 1981

Christ cared for people in their most individual needs. He cared for the widow who lost her only son. He cared for the man who was paralyzed for thirty-eight years. He cared for the blind, the woman at the well, the sick and the sinner. In the final analysis then, pastoral ministry must be rooted in that same divine love which transcends everything. This love does not encompass only man but the entire cosmos. Listen to St Isaac the Syrian speak:

What is a loving heart? It is a heart burning with love for the whole of creation, for men, for the birds, for the beasts, for the demons and all creatures. He who has such a heart cannot see or call to mind a creature without his eyes becoming filled with tears by reason of the immense compassion which seizes his heart; a heart which is offended and can no longer bear to see or learn from others of any suffering, even the smallest pain, being inflicted upon a creature. This is why such a man never ceases to pray also for animals, for the enemies of truth and for those who do him evil, that they may be preserved and purified. He will pray even for the reptiles, moved by the infinite pity which reigns in the hearts of those who are becoming united to God.

Commencement Address,
St Vladimir's Seminary, 1981

During the Renaissance period, people used to gather in salons to read poetry and discuss various intellectual and artistic trends. Today the average American comes home from work exhausted, depressed and in no mood at all to read volumes. He acquires his knowledge from watching the evening news, reading TIME Magazine and the headlines in some newspaper. His only indication of reality is the economic forecast. Despite such human conditions, the priests must proclaim the "good news." But if the priest has no news to proclaim, then he will merely add to his people's despair.

Commencement Address,
St Vladimir's Seminary, 1981

What is the priestly office? John Chrysostom describe it as follows:

The priestly office is indeed discharged on earth, but it ranks amongst heavenly ordinances; and very naturally so: for neither man, nor angels, nor archangels, nor any other created power, but the Paraclete . . . the Holy Spirit . . . Himself instituted this vocation, and persuaded men to represent the ministry of angels.

A vocation is a divine calling. A profession is to engage in a job for gain or livelihood. One could see that there is a fundamental difference between priesthood as a vocation and priesthood as a profession. A professional priest goes through the motion of prayer but does not pray. A professional priest preaches about love without any experience of what love is. A professional priest visits the sick but does not care whether they live or die.

"To the Clergy," 1978

Preach to glorify God and not yourself. People come to

church to worship God, not the priest. St Paul said: "For what we preach is not ourselves, but Jesus Christ as Lord with ourselves as your servants" (1 Cor 4:5).

Commencement Address,
St Vladimir's Seminary, 1981

What is the Church doing about our predicament? In the past sixty-five years we have built beautiful churches, cultural centers and have become very well organized both on the national and local levels. We have become experts in raising money, in business, in canon law, in constitutions and bylaws, and in golfing. We have become a Church of cookies, bake sales, raffles and lately, bingo. Is this the true mission of the Church? When the Church becomes one more institution, one more bureaucracy, will she say anything worthwhile? Can we enrich our spiritual poverty by cookies and bake sales? Can we cover our spiritual nakedness by bricks and stones?

Pittsburgh, 1970

We Orthodox are fortunate that we represent two thousand years of theology and spirituality. But where is our spiritual impact on the life of this nation? Who is articulating our Orthodox theology for the benefit of our Christian brethren who have been victimized and confused by all kinds of theological innovations? Where is our presence in the media? Where is our moral influence on our national and international politics?

"Anticipating: On the Future
of the Church in America," 1977

One of the most painful experiences in my life as your bishop, is transferring priests from one parish to another.

"To the Clergy," 1978

Mission begins with oneself, and self-evangelization means bringing the Gospel of Jesus to yourself first. If we are not converted on a personal basis, how can we convert others to Christ? Conversion to Christ is a life-long process. Striving for perfection is a constant struggle. It begins with baptism, chrismation, communion, prayer, fasting and alms-giving. St Seraphim of Sarov said: "Save yourself and thousands around you will be saved." Self-evangelization is not an easy task. It takes a great deal of discipline, soul searching, restlessness, inner-struggle and pain. It is easier to invade outer space than to invade our inner-being.

Charleston, 1978

When Doctor Trad told me that my heart operation took six hours I was amazed, thanked him for his skill and thanked God for His infinite goodness and mercy. After four days in the intensive care unit I was transferred to a private room and began to feel stronger every day. Needless to say that the days and night at the hospital were very long. The hospital world is a world of sorrow and tears, and a priest will never fully appreciate his ministry to the sick unless he suffers.

"Personal Reflections," 1972

A few months ago a Moselm mother from Lebanon, brought to my office her thirteen-year-old son, Mouawait, who is stricken with a chronic kidney disease. His mother wept and said: "If you do not help my son, he might die."

I looked at that yellow and pale face of Mouawait as if I were looking at the face of Christ. "Truly, I say unto you, as you did it to one of the least of these my brethren, you did it to me" (Matt 25:40). Sweet little Mouawait left with some hope for a healthy life. If we do not identify with the poor, the sick and the needy, regardless of creed, color, class or national background, then our Christianity must be seriously questioned. In his second Epistle to the Corinthians 11:29, St Paul said: "Who is weak, and I am not weak? Who is scandalized and I am not on fire?"

Atlanta, 1973

If you study the development of our church canon law during the first eight centuries, you will find that the Church always responded courageously to the challenges of difficult events and difficult circumstances. This means that the early Church did not live in an ivory tower indifferent to the needs of the faithful; on the contrary, the Church was very responsive to man's spiritual needs and conditions according to different times and circumstances.

Atlanta, 1973

It was revealed to us by St Peter that we are a chosen race because God has chosen us before the foundation of the world. We are a royal priesthood because Christ is the high priest and all of us share in His priesthood. We are a holy nation, God's own people, because we were "bought with a price" (1 Cor 7:23), and the price was the blood of the Lamb. Therefore, we must declare the wonderful deeds of Him who called us out of darkness into His marvelous light. The Gentiles walked in utter darkness, and in less measure the Jews; but we, as Christians, have been called out of all races, and all lands in order to be God's own people. What a privilege! And yet, what a responsibility! God took the initiative by choosing us and by allowing us to share in His priesthood. What then should our response be to Him? And, how can we declare His wonderful deeds?

"The Ministry of Laity," Toronto, 1983

We all know that Christ is the perfect priest and the suffering servant, and since we are His "own people," we are called to be the extension of His priesthood and His ministry, in time and space, whether we are clergy or laity; hence the whole body of the Church is priestly, and the whole Church is the *Laos*, the people of God. On many occasions in the past I have told you that the Church is not the bishop alone, nor the priest alone, nor the deacon alone, nor the laity alone. The Church is the bishop, the priest, the deacon and the laity ministering together like a symphony for the edification of the whole Body of Christ. Despite the existence of the ordained ministry, which is deeply rooted in the New Testament, there is "the ministry of all the believers" by virtue of their baptism. "For as many of you as were baptized into Christ have put on Christ" (Gal 3:27). For centuries the priestly nature of all the believers has been neglected and misunderstood in our Church. No wonder then, that many of our laity still exist on the margin of the Church as spectators without any significant involvement in the liturgy, discipline and ministry of the Church. Could it be that we, the clergy, have stifled the spirit of the laity and neglected their many gifts? Could it be that the hierarchical principle at the expense of the lay ministry? In his epistle to the Romans, St Paul said:

Having gifts that differ according to the grace given to us, let us use them: if prophecy, in proportion to our faith; if service, in our serving; he who teaches, in his teaching; he who exhorts, in his exhortation; he who contributes, in liberality; he who gives aid, with zeal; he who does acts of mercy, with cheerfulness (Rom 13:6-8).

"The Ministry of Laity," Toronto, 1983

This gate leads you to Calvary, and the only joy which you experience in it is the joy of the Cross. Did you experience this joy during the past year? I pray that some of you did. As for myself, I have experienced only moments of that joy. The rest of my days were full of anxiety, restlessness, and dissatisfaction. Some of you might ask: "Why are you dissatisfied? We have strong organizations, we are building churches and cultural centers, we are contributing our nickel per week to the Archdiocese and some Sundays we sell candy or we organize spaghetti dinners to help the poor." Yes, you do all these nice things, but I am still dissatisfied. I am the first among you to be condemned because of the lack of commitment on my part to the Cross of the Master. I am dissatisfied because the Inner Temple is nothing but ashes. I am dissatisfied because my nickel per week is too insignificant and not enough to support Seminarians and Seminaries, provide for the poor, and in general, to do the work and ministry of the Church. And yet, some of us think it is enough.

Miami, 1969

The clergy have the responsibility of assembling and building up the Body of Christ. They preside over the eucharistic gatherings, perform the sacraments and proclaim the Word. They exercise this authority, however, in the name of Christ. Thus their authority is not and must not be of domination and despotism. It is an authority based on love and service (Diakonia). Otherwise, it will be void of any Christian significance. In the Gospel of St Mark, our Lord said: "You know that those who are supposed to rule over the

Gentiles lord it over them and their great men exercise authority over them. But it shall not be so among you; but whoever would be great among you must be your servant, and whoever would be first among you must be slave to all," (Mark 10:42-44).

"The Ministry of Laity," Toronto, 1983

The Church does not have one theology for the clergy and another for the laity. Christ cannot be divided. After we are resurrected from the baptismal font, we receive the sacrament of chrismation through the priest who says, "the seal of the gift of the Holy Spirit." All gifts, therefore, "are inspired by one and the same spirit, who apportions to each one individually as he wills" (I Cor 12:11). We have the same spirit but different gifts, and rightly so. The members of the body are equally important; however, they perform different functions. The Apologist, Justin Martyr, restated the principle of the priesthood of all believers when he wrote, "being inflamed by the word of Christ's calling, we are the true high priestly race of God." St Clement of Rome specified what he meant by the lay ordination when he wrote, "let each of us brethren in his own order make eucharist to God, keeping a good conscience and not transgressing the appointed rule of His liturgy." In the second Christian century, St Irenaeus said, "All who are justified through Christ, have the sacred order."

Based on the witness of the Scripture and the Fathers, the laity therefore have a definite ministry to perform in the life of the Church.

"The Ministry of the Laity," Toronto, 1983

For many years we have been administering our local parishes under a false dichotomy, under a dangerous and completely un-Orthodox dualism. For many years we have been preaching two kinds of theology: one for the Church upstairs, and one for the hall downstairs. We do not believe in this upstairs-downstairs theology. Nor do we believe in the existence of two classes in the parish opposing each other: namely clergy versus laity.

Pittsburgh, 1968

This world-denying attitude, my friends, is not Christian at all. In the Gospel of St John, we read, "For God so loved the world that he gave his only begotten Son, that whoever believes in him should not perish but have eternal life," (John 3:16). If this were not so, what then was the purpose of the Incarnation? The layman, whether he is a farmer, a truck driver, a teacher, a businessman, a doctor, a lawyer, an engineer, a physicist or a scientist is much more involved in the affairs of this world than any priest. The priest's parish is limited, but the layman's parish is the whole world. It is mainly through its laity that the Church enters into contact with the world. It is at this meeting point of the Christian and non-Christian, the sacred and the profane, the religious and the secular, that the layman stands, and it is here that he encounters the problem.

"Ministry of the Laity," Toronto, 1983

The laity, however, cannot fulfill their ministry to the Church and the world if they are not regular members of the worshiping community. We need Christ-bearing (*Christophoros*) laity, conscious of their royal priestly responsibilities, to which they were called by baptismal ordination. Although we do not expect all our laity to be expert theologians, we do not expect them to be theologically illiterate. It is the sacred duty of our priests to encourage the ministry of the laity in their communities and cultivate their talents.

"Ministry of the Laity," Toronto, 1983

When we speak about the ministry of the laymen in the Church, we do not exclude the ministry of the laywomen. Women have been ministering to the Church since the inception of the early Christian community. Both the Scripture and the apostolic teachings testify to this fact. Women were the first to announce the most joyful news of the glorious Resurrection, and their icons adorn our iconostasis and walls of our churches. In his epistle to the Philippians, St Paul wrote: "And I ask you also, true yokefellow, help these women, for they have labored side by side with me in the gospel together with Clement and the rest of my fellow workers, whose names are in the book of life" (4:3). And in his epistle to the Romans, St Paul wrote: "Greet Priscilla and Aquila, my fellow co-workers in Christ Jesus, who risked their necks for my life, to whom not only I, but all the churches of the Gentiles, give thanks" (16:3-4).

"Ministry of the Laity," Toronto, 1983

In his first epistle to the Corinthians, chapter 4, verse 15, St Paul wrote: "For though you have ten thousand instructors in Christ, yet you have not many fathers." The priest then is a father to his family and not a dictator. He is the teacher of the faith and must share in the administration of the parish. He must teach his children with love, carefulness, and patience. He must understand that the priesthood is not a vacation but a vocation. He must understand that the priesthood is a martyrdom for Christ's sake.

Pittsburgh, 1968

What are the goals of missions? First, we must provide for communities of our own people who have no church but need one. This goal has priority because with each passing year the individuals in such groups drift farther and farther away from our orbit. Second, we must encourage Pan-Orthodox groups to organize parishes to serve all Orthodox people, regardless of national origin. Lastly, we must continue the policy of this Archdiocese that began in 1905 of providing for converts from the non-Orthodox world who have found the true faith.

Miami, 1969

Both the Old and the New Testament testify beyond a doubt to the important role which women played in the history of salvation. Time does not permit to speak in detail about Ruth, Sarah, Rebecca, Rachael, the Virgin Mary, the ointment bearers, the deaconesses and many others who ministered to the Church and Christ, and who were instruments of His divine purpose in history.

Therefore, it is most disappointing that in some parishes women are not allowed to vote or to be elected to Church Councils. We must definitely do away with this medieval and archaic outlook concerning women. Our Church does not teach that women are inferior to men. Despite their different functions, men and women are equal in the eyes of God because both were redeemed by His precious blood. St Paul said, "There is neither male nor female; for you are all one in Christ Jesus" (Gal 3:28).

Los Angeles, 1972

These were some of the thoughts which I desired to share with you this year. It takes hard work and clear vision to create the future. Despite our infirmities, and that "thorn in the flesh," we have come a long way in the past six years.

If it is the will of God that we continue in this sacred partnership, then may His will be done. I pray that we never lose sight of our true goals and clear visions. I also pray that we continue to dream dreams, even in the noonday, for according to Edgar Allan Poe:

Those who dream by day, are cognizant of many things which escape those who dream only by night.

Los Angeles, 1972

The *Didache*, which is a second century Christian document, tells us that one of the main functions of deacons in the early Church was to distribute the offerings of the faithful to the poor. The early Christians offered to God the fruit of their labor; they offered themselves, they offered to God what belongs to Him, and everything we have belongs to God. None of us will be able to take one penny to the grave. In II Corinthians, St Paul speaks about the way the faithful of Macedonia contributed to the poor in Jerusalem:

For they gave according to their means, as I can testify, and beyond their means, of their own free will, begging us earnestly for the favor of taking part in the relief of the saints—and this, not as we expected, but first they gave themselves to the Lord and to us by the will of God (II Cor 8:3-5).

Thus, if you give yourself to God, when you give, then your giving becomes "an expression of service, of worship and of tenderness." If you are no willing to give Him cheerfully a small portion of what He gave you, you do not deserve to be called a Christian.

Montreal, 1974

I have told you many times that the Church is not the bishop alone, nor is it the clergy or the laity alone. The Church is the bishop, the clergy and the laity working together as a beautiful symphony for the glory of God.

Louisville, 1975

St Paul describes the Church as the Body of Christ, and in this body there are many members, and each member has a specific function to perform. All members of this body are equal in the eyes of God, despite their different functions. St Paul says: "There are varieties of gifts but the same spirit: and there are varieties of service, but the same Lord; and there are varieties of working but it is the same God who inspires them all in every one. To each is given the manifestation of the spirit for the common good" (1 Cor 12:4-7). Based on this, we may rightly say that there is a difference of purpose and of service—not of nature and substance—between the priesthood of the laity and the priesthood of the clergy.

Los Angeles, 1981

During their life, Apostles kept the name "Apostle." Those, however, who they ordained and appointed to take charge and to replace them in certain localities like Philippi, Ephesus, Crete and Corinth were called "EPISCOPOI" or bishops. During the last decade of the first Christian century, St Clement of Rome dealt clearly with this subject. He reminded the Corinthians that their leaders are bishops (*EPISCOPOI*) who have succeeded the Apostles. The same concept is evident in the writings of St Irenaeus, and St Hippolytus, Bishop of Rome, and the testimony of St Ignatius, Bishop of Antioch, who considers the Christian priesthood as the highest good illustrated to man. In his Epistle to the people of Smyrna, he describes the threefold ministry of the priesthood in a way that leaves no doubt regarding the validity and historicity of the office of bishop, priest and deacon. Since we have established the Divine institution and the historicity of the EPISCOPOI, the question now is: Did the clergy and laity play any role in the election of the bishops? The answer to this question is yes, they definitely did.

There is no doubt then, that the New Testament and holy tradition give testimony to the fact that since the inception of the Church, the people have had the right to participate in the election of their bishops. We know from the history of the Church that some laymen have even participated in ecumenical and local councils and have helped formulate Christian dogmas and doctrines. From the Orthodox viewpoint, the sacrament of priesthood encompasses all the faithful, clergy and laity alike. All the members of the Body of Christ constitute "a holy nation, a chosen people and a royal priesthood" (I Peter 2:9). All of them constitute that sacred fellowship (*Koinonia Agion*). Within this all-inclusive fellowship, there is a fellowship of charismatics, a fellowship of service (*Koinonia Diakonias*) composed of deacons, priests and bishops. All those, however, who were baptized in Christ have put on Christ and were called to perform a special ministry in the life of the Church. The hierarchical principle in our Church is sometimes over-emphasized to the extent that the fellowship of service becomes obscured. Christ did not enter history, was not crucified and resurrected from the dead for the hierarchy alone, but for all the people of God (*Laos Tou Theou*), which constitute the totality (the *Pleroma*) of the Body of Christ.

"On the Election of Bishops," Los Angeles, 1981

Despite the evil days, despite the trials and tribulations of life, and despite the enemies which are on the attack from all sides, the Church will triumph because we are co-workers with Him who said: "I will build my church and the gates of hell shall not prevail against her" (Matt 16:18). Christ did not make just a visit to this earth to establish a Church and leave it to the wolves, but as the Lord of history He continues to work with us through His Holy Church which is His extension in time and space. Did He not tell us, "I will be with you until the end of time"? (Matt 28:20). St Paul admonishes us "not to accept the grace of God in vain." How important it is to remember these words.

Los Angeles, 1981

We must realize once and for all that we are on the threshold of the twenty-first century. The third millennium will be upon us more swiftly than the twinkling of an eye. The question, therefore, is: Are we prepared to face the challenges of the next century?

Boston, 1985

III

On Faith and Freedom

"Stand fast therefore in the liberty where-
with Christ has set us free. . . . For, brethren,
you have been called unto liberty; only do
not use this liberty for an occasion of sin,
but to serve one another through love."

(Gal 5:1,13)

Nothing worthwhile in this life can be achieved without struggle, and suffering will always lead to Christ if it is understood in the light of the Cross. This was the conviction of Father Alexander Schmemann. The German poet Goethe once said: "He who does not eat his bread with tears, and he who does not spend the midnight hours weeping and waiting for the dawn, does not know you, ye heavenly powers."

"On the Death of Father Schmemann," 1983

Man has never been an island unto himself. The shores of his concern have expanded from his neighborhood to his nation, and from his nation to his world. Free men have always known the necessity for responsibility. This responsibility should weigh heavily upon the hearts of all free men. Dostoevsky realized this when he wrote:

I tell you man has no more agonizing anxiety than to find someone to whom he can hand over the gift of freedom with which the unhappy creature is born.

San Francisco, 1976

Freedom without responsibility is chaos. Only *responsible* freedom is a divine gift which we must preserve and cherish and responsibly pass on to the next generation.

In October 1973, Alexander Solzhenitsyn wrote:

The most important part of our freedom, inner freedom, is always subject to our will. If we surrender it to corruption, we do not deserve to be called human.

During the past two hundred years, we have made the greatest contributions to mankind in the fields of science, technology, medicine, economics and social concerns; and we Orthodox can be justly proud of our important role in these developments. We must be cautious, however, lest we become arrogant and self-sufficient. Arrogance and self-sufficiency bear the seeds of our own destruction as individuals and ultimately as a nation.

San Francisco, 1976

Despite the doctrinal victory which the Church scored against the iconoclastic heresy of the eighth century, iconoclasm continued to challenge the Church relentlessly through many socio-economic, philosophical and political ideologies. Such ideological challenges are no longer aimed at church icons but rather at man, the real and living icon of God.

"On Contemporary Iconoclasm," Pittsburgh, 1976

The representation of Christ's divine and incomprehensible nature is beyond the realm of iconography and art. St John of Damascus profoundly stated this reality as follow: "If we made an image of the invisible God, we would certainly be in error, but we do nothing of the sort; for we are not in error if we make the image of the Incarnate God, who appeared on earth in the flesh, and who in His ineffable goodness lived with human beings and assumed the nature, the thickness, the shape and the color of the flesh." When we venerate the icon of Christ, we do not venerate wood and color, but the Creator of the universe who became matter for our salvation.

"On Contemporary Iconoclasm," Pittsburgh, 1976

The first Pan-Orthodox encyclical in the United States which was released to the press last December stated: "The Divine Liturgy was first sung on this continent three decades before the American Revolution by Orthodox pioneers who were swiftly followed by Russian missionaries bringing the faith of Jerusalem, Antioch and Byzantium to the native Americans who still cherish it." There is no doubt whatsoever that our faith is deeply rooted in the American soil.

"Anticipating: On the Future of the Church in America," 1977

Individually, Orthodox jurisdictions have done much for themselves. We have some of the finest theological institutions in the world. We have excellent religious publications. Many volumes have been written in English on Orthodox theology. We have some of the best Christian Education programs. Our clergy are highly educated and deeply committed to the Orthodox faith. We have built multimillion dollar churches and cathedrals and our laity are well organized and have contributed generously to the financial and spiritual wellbeing of our parishes. Collectively, however, we have not been able to rise above our ethnicity and work together with one mind and one accord for the glory of Orthodoxy.

Worcester, 1984

The European Renaissance inaugurated a new era of iconoclastic heresies such as godless humanism, godless Marxism and godless nationalism. These ideologies under the influence of power politics in both capitalist and communist countries tried to enslave man, reduce him to a mere tool of production and make him self-sufficient by divorcing him from God, and consequently, from a total Christian view of himself and history.

"On Contemporary Iconoclasm," Pittsburgh, 1976

In the Gospel of St John, our Lord said: "My father is working still and I am working" (John 5:17). Thus, we cannot blame God or the Holy Spirit for our inaction. History, from a Christian perspective, is a dynamic process because it is the arena of God's action in the past as well as in the present. But, if we do not fully, creatively and faithfully respond to the divine challenge, no change can be effected in our Church, values and human situation. Our forefathers, motivated by the power of the Holy Spirit, have fought valiantly and triumphantly against iconoclasm and all kinds of heresies; but the triumphalism of the past will not save us from the sterility of the present and the uncertainty of the future.

Worcester, 1984

I believe that the problem of the diaspora, this tremendous exodus of millions of Orthodox Christians from their native countries, constitutes a major and unprecedented experience in the history of the Church.

"Anticipating: On the Future of the Church in America," 1977

Sooner or later the cruel steps of history will march over our graves, so let us not waste time in vain talk and vain glory. Let us lay a firm foundation for an Orthodox spirituality in this land. In Matt 7:24-25 Christ said:

Everyone then who hears these words of mine and

does them will be like a wise man who built his house upon the rock; and the rain fell and the floods came, and the winds blew and beat upon the house, but it did not fall because it has been founded on the rock.

The floods are about us and the storms of our time are blowing very hard. If we have the strong faith of our forefathers, we can walk on the water and silence the howling wind. But if our convictions are weak, the floods and the winds will sweep us away to the oceans of oblivion.

Pittsburgh, 1970

There is a difference between contemplating history and worshiping history.

Worcester, 1984

While other Christians have focused their eyes on Calvary, we have focused ours on the empty tomb. Do we not experience this reality every year on Easter morning when we shout, "Christ is Risen from the dead?" In I Cor 15:14, 22 St Paul said:

If Christ has not been raised, then our preaching is in vain and your faith is in vain. For as in Adam all die, so also in Christ shall all be made alive.

On Great Friday, there were tears, pain, agony and death, but on the third day, the darkness of Great Friday was dissipated by the bright light of the empty tomb. The new Pascha inaugurated the new age, the new being, and the new man. The Orthodox Church celebrates this joyful event every Sunday. The following are some of the hymns which we chant on the morning of the Holy Resurrection which reveal to us this joy and this new being:

"Let us cleanse our senses that we may behold Christ shining like lightning with the unapproachable light of resurrection. That we may hear Him say openly, 'rejoice,' while we sing to Him the hymn of triumph and victory."

"Verily this day which is called 'holy' is the first day among Sabbaths, it is their King and Lord, it is the feast of feasts, and the season of seasons."

Where are those who say there is "no exit?" Let them gaze at the empty tomb. Our hope is genuine because it is rooted in the reality of the Resurrection.

Pittsburgh, 1970

During the dark ages of Orthodox theology, our Church survived because of the richness of her liturgical life. If you understand our various liturgical services, you will understand the whole theology of the Orthodox Church. While others talk about liturgical poverty and liturgical renewal, as Orthodox, we must concentrate our efforts on liturgical understanding.

Pittsburgh, 1970

We cannot acquire a mystical experience in the Church if the Liturgy is nothing but a business meeting or another lecture. A few years ago I talked to a group of non-Orthodox students about the nature of our worship. One of them asked, "Why do you not preach in the Orthodox Church?" I said, we do preach in the Orthodox Church, but we do more than that. We do not tell the faithful only what Christ said, but what He in reality did through the sacrament of the Holy Eucharist.

Pittsburgh, 1970

In the past years we have talked much about pollution of our air, our rivers, our lakes and our oceans; but nobody said a word about our inner pollution. We have breathed our inner poison in the air, we have dumped our inner garbage in the water, and unless we clean the garbage from within, that garbage from without will definitely suffocate us.

Pittsburgh, 1970

Have we reached the dead end? The "no exit" of Jean-Paul Sartre? Shall we surrender to despair, or is there hope for a better world? I am not a pessimist, nor shall I ever surrender to despair because my Church is a Church of hope. Despite the thickness of the clouds, the sun can still brightly shine. If you study the life of Christ, you will find in it moments of sadness, moments of tears, moments of tragedy and moments of joy. This is how I understand history. The Church never promised us a paradise on earth; therefore, we must reject all social Utopian thinking and accept both the blind and bright moments in history with faith, hope, dignity and courage.

Pittsburgh, 1970

In September of 1972, after spending a few days in Hillsboro, Florida with a good friend, Dr. Sayfie informed me that I needed another coronary arteriogram test. Needless to say, I was depressed to hear that because I hated to be subjected to another one of these tests. Upon examining the result of the test, Dr. Sayfie informed me that I would be operated on Monday morning September 18. Sunday, September 17, Father Antoun Khouri and my brother Najib and his wife arrived at the hospital and we spent a pleasant day recalling many beautiful past memories. Sunday afternoon Father Michael Husson was kind enough to give me Communion. Sunday evening Dr. Trad, who is a member of the surgical team, explained to me the nature of the operation. The complexity of the surgery was beyond my comprehension and when Dr. Trad asked me whether I had any questions, I simply said "no." At 10:00 PM I asked Father Antoun to recite to me Psalm 50 in Arabic,

Have mercy upon me O God according to thy great mercy. And according to the multitude of thy tender mercies blot out my iniquity. . . .

When Father Antoun finished I asked him to recite it once more and he did. Then it was time for him, Najib and Elaine to depart. After they left, a nurse came to give me a sleeping pill; I kindly thanked her and refused to take anything. I slept well until 7:00 AM when a nurse woke me up and gave me a shot to prepare me for the big operation. The last people I saw while leaving the room were Father Antoun, Najib and Elaine. I waved good-bye to them and slowly slipped into the realm of unconsciousness.

"Personal Reflections," 1972

Our modern culture is clearly marked by violence, brokenness, dislocation and rootlessness. This means that when you truly see the world, as American Orthodox Christians, you will discover that the dignity of man is threatened and that human relationships are strained by competition and suspicion. Such a world situation cries out for a Church, priests and Church people that reach out with all their energy through policies, priorities and programs into the troubled heart of the world. Yes, such a world situation demands from us a theology of reconciliation, healing and hope.

Commencement Address,
St Vladimir's Seminary, 1981

The Church in the new world must observe three basic facts: When, where and to whom; time, place and people. We are neither in Byzantium nor in Imperial Russia. We are in the United States of America and on the threshold of a new century.

Commencement Address,
St Vladimir's Seminary, 1981

Now the question is, what form or direction does Jesus' revolution take? Did He advocate bloodshed, violence, burning, destruction, hate and animosity in order to reform society and abolish social injustice? The answer to this question can be easily found in the Gospels "... do violence to no man, neither accuse any falsely" (Luke 3:14); "Then Jesus said unto him, 'put up again thy sword into its place for all they that take by the sword shall perish with the sword'" (Matt 26:52); "Ye have heard that it hath been said, 'an eye for an eye, and a tooth for a tooth.' But I say unto you that ye resist not evil but whosoever shall smite thee on thy right cheek, turn to him the other also" (Matt 6:38-39); "Blessed are the peacemakers for they shall be called the children of God" (Matt 2:9); "Recompense to no man evil for evil. Provide things honest in the sight of all men" (Rom 12:17).

"Christ, Social Justice and Violence," 1979

The New Testament never ignored man and his social

problems. I believe that Jesus was, still is and will continue until the end of time to be the most dynamic revolutionary figure in history. In His disdain for social injustice He uttered the strongest terms against the Scribes and Pharisees. He never tolerated nor condoned evil.

Dietrich Bonhoeffer, a German theologian, knew this when he wrote:

There are people who are regarded as frivolous, and some Christians think it impious for anyone to hope and prepare for a better earthly future. They think that the meaning of present events is chaos, disorder catastrophe; and in resignation or pious escapism they surrender all responsibility for reconstruction and for future generations. It may be that the day of judgement will dawn tomorrow, and in that case not before we shall gladly stop working for a better future.

The same author asks, "Are we still of any use?" This is the way he answers his own question:

We have been silent witnesses of evil deeds; we have been drenched by many storms; are we still of any use? What we shall need is not geniuses, or cynics, or clever tacticians, but plain, honest and straightforward men. Will our inward power of resistance be strong enough, and our honesty with ourselves remorseless enough for us to find our way back to simplicity and straightforwardness? (Letters from Prison, 16-17)

"Christ, Social Justice and Violence," 1979

The European Christian, against all Christian teaching, has exploited other races throughout history—especially in Africa and Asia by means of colonization and economic abuse. Today Asia is revolting and Africa is awakening, and it is time for the white people to realize once and for all that they are but a small minority among the races of the world. Woe to them if they do not stop taking advantage of these under-developed nations! The Incarnate Logos did not assume only the nature of the white race, but the entire nature of man, except sin, regardless of whether or not man was white, black or yellow.

"Christ, Social Justice and Violence," 1979

God loved man and this is precisely why He entered history; this is why eternity invaded time and heaven embraced the earth. It was indeed a sad day when Adam and Eve left paradise. One of the Church Fathers said, "When Adam and Eve left Paradise they saw the sunset for the first time." According to the Gospel of Saint John, "the Word became flesh" (John 1:2) so that the sun which Adam and Eve saw setting, may shine forever.

"Christ, Social Justice and Violence," 1979

On many occasions we hear Christ through the Gospels admonishing the rich to share their wealth with the poor. When He shall come again in His glory to judge the world, He will judge us according to our faith and deeds.

"Christ, Social Justice and Violence," 1979

The most explosive, the most devastating and the most cancerous enigma which confronts our society today is racism. This problem is deeply rooted in the history of the United States, and it will never be solved by legislation and demonstration, nor by looting, shooting, burning, and destruction. The tragic relations of black and white people in this country lie not in the structure of the economic system, nor in the mountains, nor streams, nor valleys, and neither in the hamlets and cities of our great nation; it lies in the heart and conscience of the American people.

"Christ, Social Justice and Violence," 1979

Where do we as Orthodox Christians stand *vis-a-vis* all these tragic events? What does God and the Church teach us about social justice, racism, revolution, and violence? According to our Orthodox theology, we fundamentally and drastically disagree with the present trend of the so-called theology of violence. This does not mean that we do not have anything to say about the many social ills which are plaguing our society in this most dangerous curve of our history. We must strongly condemn racism, segregation, and the exploitation of the poor.

"Christ, Social Justice and Violence," 1979

Before the industrial and technological revolutions women had a defined role to play and a strong sense of belonging. They were deeply rooted in the family, which was in reality their kingdom. But that same industrial and technological revolution definitely changed and enlarged the role of women in life, and involved them deeply in many social affairs.

"On Women and Christianity," 1983

My mother was not a philosopher nor a soldier, but she was a poet in her own right. She opened my eyes to the beauty of life, to the holiness of the holy, and above all, she taught me how to serve and how to love others. She gave herself totally to us, expecting nothing in return. Does a nightingale expect anything in return for her singing? Does a rose expect anything in return for its fragrance? This is my mother and your mother—this is true womanhood.

"On Women and Christianity," 1983

Satan took a man and discovered Him to be God. Hell claimed earth and came face to face with heaven. This is the freedom won in Christ's Resurrection, and this is the basis for our faith, that "Death is swallowed up in victory. O Death, where is thy sting? O Hell, where is thy victory?" (I Corinthians 15:55). Since we are members of His body, we too share in His victory, "for in Jesus Christ we are all children of God, through faith. For as many as have been baptized into Christ, have put on Christ" (Galatians 3:26-27).

Brooklyn, 1974

The New Testament gave women a greater role in the history of salvation; they became equal to man in their responsibilities to the Church. St Paul said in Christ's Kingdom "There are no males or females, because all are one."

The most important personality among the New Testament women is the Theotokos, and she was given many titles, such as "Second Eve," "Queen of Heaven," and "Blessed Among Women."

"On Women and Christianity," 1983

On Golgotha Satan saw himself victorious over the very Son of God! But this demonic jubilation was premature. For although the battle on Golgotha was over, the war itself was not finished. No sooner had hell claimed the soul of Jesus Christ, than Satan discovered to his horror that he was attempting to rule the ruler, and contain the uncontainable:

Today hell cries out groaning: My power has been swallowed up; for the Shepherd, who was crucified, has raised Adam; and those whom I had swallowed, by my might, I have given up completely; for the Crucified One has emptied the graves, and the might of death has vanished. (Great Saturday)

Brooklyn, 1974

Although the Virgin Mary does not say much in the Gospel, yet she speaks to us silently about faith through her irresistible impact on the life of the Church.

"On Women and Christianity," 1983

During Holy Week the time for patient teaching and subtleties comes to an end. Now He speaks with forthright boldness, and attacks the scribes and pharisees as "hypocrites" and "sons of vipers" because they thwarted the work of God by enslaving mankind with impossible laws, while forgetting the precepts of love and mercy. But He is alone with His Father. He has no human ally. This reminds us that Christ *alone* has won this battle of freedom from death for us, and this is why He alone is the basis of the Christian faith. Christ is alone as He prays in Gethsemane. Christ is alone as He stands before the high priest. Christ is alone as He is judged by Pilate and the jeering crowd. Christ is alone as He is buffeted and mocked. Christ is alone as He carries His cross to Golgotha. Christ is alone as He suffers and dies upon the cross.

Brooklyn, 1974

Upon confronting death through the death of His friend

Lazarus, Jesus wept. But let us understand that these tears were not merely tears of mourning, but the tears which were shed by God at the sight of Man—who was created to be the king of His earthly creation—now subjected to the indignity of death and corruption. Man, who was created by God in His own image and likeness, was held captive in hell, the realm of Satan and his hosts. At this point, we can feel the tension, as the battle lines are clearly drawn. We can almost hear Christ shouting, "Enough is enough!" when He stands before the tomb of Lazarus, and commands him to arise and come forth. He, Jesus Christ, the Son of God, is the master—not Satan. And Lazarus, a symbol of all mankind, is His, Christ's creation. Jesus, not Satan, is the Lord and King of heaven and earth and has thus won the battle of freedom.

Brooklyn, 1974

This joyous proclamation "Christ is Risen!" which resounds throughout the world is the sermon of sermons, for "if Christ has not been raised, then our preaching is in vain, and your faith is in vain" (I Corinthians 15:14). The Resurrection of our Lord and Savior Jesus Christ, which Orthodox Christians joyfully announce, is the cornerstone which has set us free and upon which our faith is built.

Brooklyn, 1974

Jesus Christ, the New Man—the Second Adam—won for us the ultimate victory over evil, by overcoming and destroying Satan's most powerful and final weapon—death. Jesus Christ, the only-begotten Son of God, who was incarnate of the Holy Spirit and the Virgin Mary, became man precisely for this purpose—to do battle with Satan for us—to reclaim His creation, to free us from sin and the power of death. Indeed, He *is* our freedom.

Brooklyn, 1974

The Church of Christ is attacked by many enemies from without and within. We can overcome all these enemies if we understand the wealth, the strength, and the depth of our faith. Whatever we do during our early pilgrimage must help us life up our hearts unto the Lord. Every step we make must lead us toward heaven and we have the free will to do so.

Pittsburgh, 1968

We say the Holy Spirit is creative, inspiring, life-giving, but we try to domesticate Him and keep Him caged and limited. We must communicate the Spirit, stir up the grace that is in us. Remember, we are the successors of the Apostles, the messengers of God, and mission is the channel for this life with the Spirit.

Miami, 1969

I am not a pessimist; therefore, I do not believe in dead ends nor do I surrender to despair. Kierkegaard once said: "To move toward the light requires a leap into the dark." I am sure that after the dark night, a new day will dawn on us with everlasting light. We should never surrender to apathy. Apathetic men accomplish nothing. Someone said, "Men who believe in nothing, change nothing and renew nothing."

Boston, 1971

A marginal Christian is no Christian at all.

Atlanta, 1973

Every local parish is in reality the concrete expression of

the one Holy Catholic and Apostolic Church. The Church receives her life from above, from the "Comforter," the Spirit of Truth, who is in all places and fills all things. The Book of Acts states:

When the day of Pentecost had come, they were all together in one place. And suddenly a sound came from Heaven like the rush of mighty wind, and filled all the house where they were sitting. And there appeared to them tongues as of fire, distributed and resting on each one of them. And they were all filled with the Holy Spirit and began to speak in other tongues, as the Spirit gave them utterance (Acts 2:2-4).

The Church is not only a sociological entity, but it is—and this is most important—*a theological* reality. The parish was not created by Robert's *Rules of Order*, but by Christ Himself, who is in our midst and said, "Lo, I am with you always unto the end of the world."

Montreal, 1974

In the past ten years we have reached many goals. However, we will never reach our final goal "until we all attain to the unity of the faith and of the knowledge of the Son of God, to mature manhood, to the measure of the stature of the fullness of Christ" (Eph 4:13).

Twenty-five years ago, writing about life, I said: "Every time we climb a summit, we discover more summits to be climbed." Nikos Kazantzakis put it this way, "There is no summit, there is only height. There is no rest." The Church teaches us that man is always becoming. Our vision of the future, therefore, is to continue struggling and to continue climbing. St Paul said to the Philippians:

Finally, brethren, whatever is true, whatever is honourable, whatever is just, whatever is pure, whatever is lovely, whatever is gracious, if there is any excellence, if there is anything worthy of praise, think about these things. What you have learned and received and heard and seen in me, do: and the God of peace will be with you (Phil 4:8-9).

On His Tenth Anniversary, San Francisco, 1976

IV

On Orthodoxy and America

"Then opened He their understanding, that they might understand the scriptures, and He said to them, 'Thus it is written, and thus it behooved Christ to suffer, and to rise from the dead the third day: And that repentance and remission of sins should be preached in His name among all nations, beginning at Jerusalem. And you are witnesses of these things."

(Luke 24:45-48)

During the first one thousand years of her existence, the Church was courageous enough to respond to the challenges of her time. Many local councils were called and seven ecumenical councils were convened to deal with important issues which the Church had to face. The question now is: What happened to that dynamism which characterized the life of the Church between Pentecost and the tenth century? Did God stop speaking to the Church? Did the action of the Holy Spirit in the Church cease after the tenth century? Why are we always celebrating the remote past? Have we been lost in our long, long history? I wish we could gather to celebrate an event which happened five hundred years ago or two hundred years ago, or perhaps, something which happened last year!

Worcester, 1984

Despite our rootedness in the American soil, our Church in America is still divided into more than fourteen jurisdictions, contrary to our Orthodox ecclesiology and Canon Law which forbid the multiplicity of jurisdictions in the same territory.

Worcester, 1984

We have much to offer to America. We can offer America two thousand years of spirituality in a language which America understands. Instead of Transcendental Meditation we can offer Orthodoxy, St Simeon the New Theologian, St John Chrysostom and St Basil the Great. We have been on this continent for more than a century selfishly enjoying our

83

ethnic traditions and talking to America in languages which
America does not understand. No wonder then, that despite
the depth of our spirituality which this pragmatic culture
badly needs, we have not been able to leave any spiritual
impact on the life of this nation.

"On Contemporary Iconoclasm," Pittsburgh, 1976

We Orthodox have a tendency, especially on the Sunday
of Orthodoxy, to glorify the past and feel proud of ourselves.
There is no doubt that the Church of the Ecumenical Councils
was glorious and courageous because she responded to the
challenges of her time. Have we responded to the challenges
of our time? As individual jurisdictions, I believe that we
have succeeded in building new churches, in educating young
priests and in organizing choirs and church schools; but collectively, we have done absolutely nothing.

"On Contemporary Iconoclasm," Pittsburgh, 1976

During the past two centuries we have witnessed the
reduction of man into small entities such as science, technology, sex and economics. Today the western man has become "mechanized, routinized and made comfortable as an
object."

A French poet recently said:

Why are the times so dark
Men know each other not at all
Governments clearly change from bad to worse
Days dead and gone were more worthwhile,
Now what holds sway? Deep gloom and boredom
Justice and law nowhere to be found
I know no more where I belong.

Is the cry of this poet not our own cry? Do we belong any-where? Do we belong to the Church in the true sense of belonging? Do we represent any view at all concerning man and his destiny? Do we encounter God in our worship, medi-tation and tragedy? Man truly know himself when he is confronted by God.

Pittsburgh, 1970

I appeal to you in the name of everything which we represent to join me in a glorious venture for an Orthodox future of hope, joy and fulfillment. We have tarried long enough on the shore. It is time to sail and plunge into the depths.

Pittsburgh, 1970

We cannot be agents of change in full obedience to the truth unless we transcend ethnicism and establish a new Orthodox reality in North America. I am not asking you to deny your own history and your own culture. What I am asking is to blend your old and new cultures into some kind of an integrated reality. I am not against ethnicism, if ethnicism means a return to the spirit of the Desert Fathers, the Syrian Fathers, the Greek Fathers, and the Slavic Fathers. But if ethnicism means a narrow, fanatic, ghetto mentality which separates us from each other, then I am definitely against such ethnicism.

Worcester, 1984

The words of the late Alexander Schmemann speak best to our contemporary hope in America: "One can almost visual-ize the glorious and blessed day when forty Orthodox bishops of America will open their first Synod in New York, or Chicago or Pittsburgh with the hymn, 'Today the grace of the Holy Spirit assembled us together,' and will appear to us not as 'representatives' of Greek, Russian or any other 'jurisdictions' and interest, but as the very icon, the very 'Epiphany' of our unity within the Body of Christ; when each of them and all together will think and deliberate only in terms of the whole, putting aside all particular and national problems, real and important as they may be. On that day, we shall 'taste and see' the oneness of the Orthodox Church in America."

Worcester, 1984

The last time I heard his distinct voice was two days before he went to the hospital in Boston, Mass. When I asked him how he felt, for the first time I heard Metropolitan Antony say, "I do not feel well." He was a man full of confidence in his physical and mental health, and death was the farthest thing from his mind. The Orthodox in America lost a great leader. His death in Boston was a tremendous emotional shock to me because I loved the man and admired him for his many excellent qualities.

"On the Death of Metropolitan Antony," 1970

Although he was not a perfect man by any means, no one can deny his tremendous contribution to the growth of our Church in North America between 1936 and 1966. On a gloomy and cold day of February 1966, with much tears and sorrow, we buried Antony on a hill overlooking the city of Brooklyn where he spent most of his years.

"On the Death of Metropolitan Antony," 1970

Most of our Orthodox people in this land are still on the

boundary, arguing whether God understands English or not. How can we reach the heart of this nation if we continue to chew the past and speak to our youth a language which they do not understand?

Pittsburgh, 1970

For the Lord your God is bringing you into a good land, a land of brooks of water, of fountains and springs, flowing valleys and hills, a land of wheat and barley.... And you shall eat and be full, and you shall bless the Lord your God for the good land He has given you.

It was this love of freedom which motivated the early pioneers to take such risks and suffer hardships. They did not want riches or fame; it was their ambition only to build themselves homes, to educate their children in the traditions of the motherland, and to worship God as their conscience dictated. They decided that in all the world America was the one place which offered them these opportunities. It is evident, therefore, that the first era of our early history was marked by fierce struggle for mere existence.

San Francisco, 1976

What is man that thou art mindful of him, and the son of man that thou dost care for him? Yet thou has made him little less than the angels, and dost crown him with glory and honor. Thou has given him dominion over the works of thy hands. Thou has put all things under his feet (Psalm 8:4-6).

Based on this divine revelation, the right of the individual to seek freedom, justice and equality, regardless of creed, race or color is very sacred. We must thank the Almighty

God that we Americans are enjoying a great measure of freedom, justice and equality. Because of our human weakness, however, we have a tendency to use our freedom to the detriment of others. My freedom ends where your freedom begins. Freedom must not become a license to deprive others and monopolize the wealth of the world at the expense of the poor. If there is a starving child in America, this means that all Americans are starving. And if there is a starving child in this world, this means that the entire world is starving. St Paul said: "Who is weak, and I am not weak? Who is made to fall, and I am not indignant?" (II Corinthians 11:29).

San Francisco, 1976

Christ's commandment to "go and make disciples of all nations," is true today as it was yesterday and it shall be until the end of history. Those of us who neglect this commandment betray the essence of the Christian message. Unfortunately, many Orthodox people are very parochial in their concept of the Church. They cannot distinguish between the parish and the Church universal. They imagine that the Church, the whole Church, is the four walls where they worship on Sunday and everything else is none of their business.

Charleston, 1978

It is not enough to build beautiful and adequate facilities for the Church to meet and glorify God. To revitalize our communities in America means to bring each and everyone in the parish to the fellowship of Christ. In the Book of Acts, St. Paul said: "And He commanded us to preach to the people, and to testify that He is the one ordained by God to be judge of the living and the dead."

Charleston, 1978

Many nations and empires have risen, flourished and collapsed because of arrogance and moral decadence. Edward Gibbon in his famous work, *The Decline and Fall of the Roman Empire,* cited five reasons why the great Roman Empire withered and died. Here are the factors he cited:

1. The undermining of the dignity and sanctity of the home—the very basis of human society.

2. Higher and higher taxes; the spending of public money for free bread and circuses for the populace.

3. The mad craze for pleasure; sports and other entertainment becoming every year more and more exciting, more brutal and more immoral.

4. The building of great armaments when the real enemy was within . . . the decay of individual responsibility.

5. The declining of religion—faith fading into mere form; losing touch with life, losing power to guide the people.

Can we read in America, today, some of these signs which Edward Gibbon painted hundreds of years ago about the collapse of the Roman Empire? Let us pray that our Great Republic will never have the same fate.

San Francisco, 1976

It is the Christian who is to affirm his deep faith in God, the Lord of History, who controls with His mighty hand the destiny of nations and empires. Without God, everything which we have built throughout the years will be consumed by fire and turn into dust and ashes. Let us never forget God's words in Deuteronomy:

You shall remember the Lord your God, for it is He who gives you power to get wealth; that He may confirm His covenant which He swore to your fathers, as at this day. And if you forget the Lord your God and go after other gods and serve them and worship them, I solemnly warn you this day that you will surely perish (Deut. 8:18-20)

San Francisco, 1976

Unfortunately, there is a tendency in the Orthodox Church to be apathetic towards the world and its social problem, and this is true especially in America. I do not find any biblical foundation for such a trend in our theology. Christ was very much involved with man and his problems. His greatness lies in the fact that He identified Himself with the poor, the slave, the oppressed, the sorrowful, and the despised. He did not only identify himself with such people but He went further than that: He died for them and for all men.

"Christ, Social Justice, and Violence," 1979

I believe that the apostles of eighteenth and nineteenth century socialism could have learned a great deal from the Church Fathers who never hesitated to demonstrate with all honesty and simplicity that we are indeed our brothers' keepers. Unfortunately, we in America are living today in the age of the de-Christianization and de-humanization of man. Man has become nothing but an object which can be eliminated if you are powerful enough to make yourself comfortable. We have reached the point where my existence seems to be the limitations of yours.

"Christ, Social Justice, and Violence," 1979

On December 1st, at the end of the dinner with the

Board of Trustees of St Vladimir's Seminary, knowing perhaps that his days on this earth were numbered, Father Schmemann spoke to us in simple and direct words which I am sure penetrated every heart. He was too ill to meet with us, and his words were reminiscent of St Paul's words recorded in II Timothy (4:6-8). "I am already on the point of being sacrificed; the time of my departure has come. I have fought the good fight, I have finished the race, I have kept the faith." Father Schmemann's words to us were his will and testament. "I am sorry," he said, "that I cannot meet with you tonight. Please take good care of the Seminary. Remember our humble beginning and how hard we fought to be where we are today." Father Schmemann uttered these words, then excused himself and vanished into the darkness of the night. There were misty eyes in the room and a strong, silent determination that the seminary will live and that the torch which Father Schmemann has lighted on this holy hill will never be extinguished.

"On the Death of Father Schmemann," 1983

Farewell, my dear friend, I am sure you have already heard these divine words. "Well done, thou good and faithful servant; you have been faithful over a little. I will set you over much; enter into the joy of your Master" (Matt 25:21).

"On the Death of Father Schmemann," 1983

I honestly do not know of any contemporary Orthodox theologian who has left more impact on our theology, spiritual lives and thought in America than Alexander Schmemann. "Whosoever shall do and teach, the same shall be called great in the kingdom of heaven" (Matt 5:19). Certainly his untimely departure shocked all of us, but in the final analysis, it is not how long we live, it is rather how deeply we live, how many candles we light and how many chapters we write in the Book of Life.

"On the Death of Father Schmemann," 1983

Since the beginning of my episcopate, Father Schmemann and I have developed a very deep friendship and have shared many, many intimate thoughts about the Seminary and the future of Orthodoxy in this hemisphere. Oh, how hard he worked and preached about Orthodoxy in this land. His burning desire was to see Orthodoxy organically united in North America. Unfortunately, he died before the realization of his dream. We shall continue to struggle for this unity and we shall dedicate our efforts to the blessed memory of Father Alexander Schmemann.

"On the Death of Father Schmemann," 1983

You might ask, what is the reason behind this Orthodox stagnation? Did our history freeze after 787 A.D.? There is no doubt that the rise of Islam, the collapse of the Byzantine Empire, and the fall of Czarist Russia have contributed much to our past and present stagnation. The sad condition of our Mother Churches across the ocean is indicative of this reality. The Patriarchate of Jerusalem is living under the heel of a Zionist state, while the Coptic Orthodox Patriarch of Egypt is still living under the yoke of a heavy government hand. And, what can I say about Antioch? If I may slightly adapt the biblical words, I would say the following: "A voice was heard in Lebanon, wailing and lamentation—Antioch weeping for her children; she refused to be consoled because they were no more" (Matt 2:18). The Church of Cyprus is suffering the consequences of a badly and sadly divided island. The Ecumenical Patriarchate is slowly, but surely, dying from Turkish oppression. Furthermore, the Patriarchate of Moscow and those of Eastern Europe continue to suffer under the yoke of communism. Have we then lost all hope for an Orthodox renaissance? Is there not a place on this planet where we can dream of a better Orthodox future? I believe that there is a place, and this place is the North American continent.

Worcester, 1984

Beyond a doubt, we are not a Church of immigrants any longer. On the contrary, I feel that we are deeply rooted in this land; thus the religious, social and intellectual trends which affect this entire society definitely leave their marks on our souls.

Worcester, 1984

We have a tremendous opportunity in this land to dream dreams and see visions; if only we can put our house in order.

Worcester, 1984

Where in the whole world, today, can you find seven million free Orthodox except in North America? We are no longer a Church of immigrants; the first Orthodox Liturgy was celebrated in this country before the American Revolution. Many of our Orthodox young people have died on the battlefields of various wars, defending American ideals and principles.

Worcester, 1984

There is so much confusion today on the American religious scene. Some of the so-called evangelists in this country are making a mockery of religion and yet they are very popular. They preach what the people want to hear, not what the people should hear. A few weeks ago, I watched *Sixty Minutes*, a CBS television program. A segment of the program was dedicated to some new evangelical trends; mainly, preaching Americanism, capitalism, and the pursuit of happiness; in other words, make people feel good and you will have a large audience and you become a successful preacher. Sweeten Christ, package Him nicely, advertise Him well, and surely you will become a multi-millionaire. Did Peter, Paul, Barnabas, Stephen and Ignatius of Antioch preach that way? Did our Lord, Himself, preach the Gospel to make people feel good? Not at all! Listen carefully to the Gospels of the first three evenings of Holy Week. I have mentioned these facts to show you the tremendous missionary task which lies ahead of us. The truth is that millions of people in this country are thirsty for the "living water" and the "heavenly bread," which are treasured in the Orthodox Church.

Charleston, 1976

Confronted with the contemporary scene in America, there are those who suggest that we withdraw and pray for the Second Advent, for we can have little direct impact on these issues. It is a worldly enterprise; therefore, to demonstrate our commitment to Christ, we must be detached, withdrawn and isolated. And then there are those who are tempted to reduce the Gospel of Jesus Christ into nothing but social activism. Consequently, prayer, self-renewal, sacraments, contemplation and spirituality are not to be taken seriously. In my humble opinion, both attitudes contradict the Gospel and the experience of the Church throughout history. And as for the priest, his great task is to live and help others to live in this tension between both attitudes and search for a synthesis. The priest is called upon to be a man of prayer, and a social reformer who does not lose his soul, "For what shall profit a man if he shall gain the whole world and loses his own soul?" (Mark 8:36). The priest is called upon to be a man of action and a man of prayer at the same time. There is hardly a doubt that being a priest calls for careful preparation, not only in terms of the knowledge and understanding of the Scripture and the sacramental life of the Church, but also in terms of the various means through which Divine Grace and God's word come to man.

Commencement Address,
St Vladimir's Seminary, 1981

In America the bishop must be very much involved in the life of his sheep. Otherwise, the word "shepherd" becomes completely meaningless. The complexity of modern life, the many serious problems which we encounter in ministering to our Orthodox people, the loneliness, cynicism and even despair which some of us experience from time to time, raise a very important question concerning our priestly image, or call it "identity." Who are we? And, what are we doing? Are we not a "royal priesthood and a chosen generation," called by God to realize His divine purpose in history? Do we know where we are going? Do we have a sense of purpose, a sense of direction?

"To the Clergy," 1978

Despite this reality we cannot consider this present Orthodox situation in America as final because, by so doing, we will betray Orthodoxy and her basic principles. I believe that we can achieve administrative unity despite our cultural diversity. The first step toward this goal would be the elevation of the Standing Conference—which has already served its purpose—to the rank of a Synod with the blessings of the Mother Churches. Such a Synod will be able to speak to America and the world with one voice and one accord. This Synod which will truly represent six million free Orthodox will be able to respond effectively to the moral and social challenges of our time.

"Anticipating: On the Future of Church in America," 1977

I am dissatisfied with the progress towards a united Orthodox Church in America. At our request last January, we met with some Orthodox hierarchs and theologians to discuss the prospects of one united Orthodox Church in America. The meeting was very fruitful, except that it was not followed up by more meetings, and when the Executive Secretary of our Archdiocese called the hierarch who promised to host the second meeting to remind him of his promise, the answer was, "We have no time." So do not be deceived when you read in some Orthodox magazines that we of the Antiochian Archdiocese are taking the passive role in the process of Orthodox unity in America.

Miami, 1969

Where do we go from here?

We Orthodox Christians have a strong tendency to glorify the past and occupy ourselves entirely with history. I am not suggesting that we should forget the past. What I am saying is that we must consult the past only to serve the present and the future. I could care less about the first Rome, second Rome and third Rome. These are political titles completely void of any theological significance. Canon 27 of the Fourth Ecumenical Council lost its meaning after the fall of Constantinople. Third Rome and Holy Russia ceased to be living realities after the 1917 Communist Revolution. Someone has said that the last act of a dying organization is to get out a new and enlarged edition of the rule book.

Pittsburgh, 1971

Faithful of this Archdiocese, we have reached the eleventh hour. A fragmented Orthodoxy in America can no longer be tolerated and can no longer survive. Our young people are tormented by our division and ghetto mentality. We must realize once and for all that, as members of the Body of Christ, we are not citizens of any country except the heavenly Jerusalem where "there can not be Greek and Jew, circumcised and uncircumcised, barbarian, Scithian, slave, freeman, but Christ is all and in all" (Colossians 3:11).

Pittsburgh, 1974

Since I came to this country twenty-five years ago, our annual conventions have been adopting resolutions in favor of Orthodox unity in America. Early this year, and in response to your mandate of past years, Metropolitan Theodosius, Primate of the Orthodox Church in America and I have appointed a bilateral commission to discuss ways and means of increased cooperation and eventual unity between our two jurisdictions which share similar visions for the future. I made it clear to the Orthodox Church in America that this Archdiocese will not take a major step in this direction without full consultation with the Holy Synod of Antioch. This commission has already met twice and many important issues are being discussed. Orthodox unity in America, however, cannot be achieved in one day; therefore, we ask you to be patient with us and pray that "all may be one."

Los Angeles, 1981

I am sorry to report to you that some Orthodox hierarchs in this country and abroad are displeased with this commission and their displeasure was officially conveyed to the Patriarchate of Antioch. I do not understand the reason behind their displeasure. If they can dialogue with the Jews about

Christian-Jewish unity, and if they can dialogue with the Roman Catholic Church and all kinds of Christian sects all over the world, is it sinful for us to dialogue with our Orthodox brothers and sisters in this country? The people of this Archdiocese are not slaves to anyone. Thus, we shall continue the work of this commission until our shameful division is overcome and Orthodox unity is realized. For a long time, the Orthodox Church has been victimized by an outdated and irrelevant feud between Moscow and Constantinople, which are still suffering from the complex of a second and third Rome that no longer exist. Unfortunately, nothing is happening in world Orthodoxy because of this continuing squabble. There is an Arabic proverb which says: "While the ship is sinking, the crew is busy painting the chimney."

Los Angeles, 1981

In America, we are in the process of developing our own schools of architecture, iconography, hymnology and theology. But, where do we go from here? It is true, Your Beatitude, that the roots are in Antioch, Jerusalem, Constantinople, Greece, Eastern Europe, and Russia; but the branches are here, and these branches are very deeply rooted in this fertile and beautiful North American soil. We will never forget our roots; what we are seeking is unity with diversity.

Your Beatitude, all the Orthodox in North America, regardless of national background, look up to you for guidance and leadership. They have been very encouraged by the positive statements which you have made *vis-a-vis* Orthodox unity on this continent. With all my respect for all Orthodox Patriarchs, you are the only Patriarch in the world today who has enough freedom and courage to dialogue sincerely and effectively with both the Greeks and Slavs. Antioch, as you well stated, does not have the "illusions of the first, second or third Rome." Being fully cognizant of this reality, please permit me to borrow an expression from the President of our country and ask you, "If not you, who? And if not now, when?"

We Orthodox represent two thousand years of history. History can be a blessing if we penetrate its depth, or it can be a curse if we permit ourselves to be crushed by its weight. Modern Orthodox history leaves much to be desired. We have been chewing the past, imitating and reiterating. We are so afraid of writing a new song, seeing a new vision and creating a new day. We have imprisoned Christ in our icons, in our temples, in our libraries and in our rituals. Paul Evdokimov, writing about modern Orthodox spirituality, said: "Its dynamism has taken refuge in national and juridical provincialism, the aestheticism of the elite, and the folk superstition of the masses. As soon as Orthodoxy hinders the forward movement of tradition, it degenerates into an immobile traditionalism and betrays its vocation." The biggest disappointment during the thirteen years of my episcopate has been the lack of sincerity and genuine interest in inter-Orthodox relations.

Your Beatitude,

Regarding the diaspora, your people in North America have always championed the cause of Orthodox unity and we shall not in any way abandon this struggle. In one of your epistles to our people, you said: "As Antiochians, our hope for Orthodox unity in North America is that it be realized with the blessings of the Mother Churches which have branches on the North American continent. A unity achieved in this fashion will be solid, strong and productive. This is our conviction and we shall continue to work for its actualization . . . we should never forget that Antioch must play a great role in peace, love and good will."

This is a great statement, your Beatitude. This is our conviction, too. Now we must work together to translate our convictions into realities. Antioch must play a great role in world Orthodoxy especially in the forthcoming "Great Synod." Among all the Orthodox patriarchates in the world, Antioch is the only patriarchate which can act freely, positively and effectively. We Antiochians have never fixed our eyes on any particular piece of land nor have we ever become slaves to any particular culture. We always believed "in one holy, catholic and Apostolic Church," a catholicity which transcends all frontiers and all cultures. Orthodoxy in the diaspora, and otherwise, has long been victimized by an historical tension between Moscow and Constantinople. It is time, your Beatitude, to put an end to this "Cold War." It is time, your Beatitude, to rise above historical considerations which no longer exist either in Moscow or Constantinople. Only a strong Antioch can play this positive role. The Patriarch of Antioch cannot be stronger than the people of Antioch; therefore, this Archdiocese which loves you and respects you, puts all its potentialities in your hands as you struggle to bring Orthodox unity to this continent and Orthodox cooperation throughout the world.

"Addressing Patriarch Elias IV,"
Washington, D.C. 1977

I believe that this unity is the greatest event which has taken place in the life of the Antiochian Patriarchate, and perhaps in the life of Orthodoxy in the hemisphere. Let us not lose sight, however, of the fact that our Antiochian unity is not an end by itself. Let us not forget that Orthodoxy on this continent is administratively divided by ethnic barriers. Such division is nothing but a judgment on all of us. Let us pray that our Antiochian unity will inspire other Orthodox ethnic jurisdictions to emulate our example and unite among themselves as a first step toward total Orthodox unity. The unity of six million Orthodox in this hemisphere remains one of our ultimate goals and we shall never rest until this goal is achieved.

"On the Unity of the Antiochian Archdiocese
in America," San Francisco, 1976

We have not made any serious impact on the spiritual and moral life of this nation because of our ethnic division. The multiplicity of jurisdictions in one given territory fundamentally contradicts the canonical and ecclesiological teachings of our Church. Orthodoxy in its essence transcends ethnicism and nationalism. Thus, if we don't destroy these ethnic barriers and feel at home in America, we will remain, in the eyes of our fellow Americans, some kind of an oriental cult or a museum for ancient relics. We have a tremendous opportunity to preach Orthodoxy in this land. America is thirsty for our spirituality and theological stability, but how can America understand us if we continue talking to her in languages which she does not understand. I am not against ethnic cultures at all. I believe that we can achieve Orthodox unity despite our cultural diversity.

"Addressing Patriarch Elias IV,"
Washington, D.C. 1977

v

On the New and Old World

"Then said He to them, 'Therefore every scribe which is instructed unto the kingdom of heaven, is like the man that is a householder, who brings forth out of his storehouse, things new and things old.'"

(Matt 13:52)

If our fathers and grandfathers traveled to the New World in the 1880's and 1890's as passengers, they were subjected to excessive heat and excessive cold. Very often, too, the ship would leave them in a country other than that of their destination. The luckiest person was the one who was met at the port by somebody waiting for him, or who had the address of a friend, or who possessed a letter of recommendation addressed to a person able to find him a room for the first night. But when they did arrive to this beautiful country it was with tears in their eyes and hope in their hearts. Tears, because they have left behind wives, children and relatives; and hope, because in America, there were still frontiers to explore, room to expand and new directions to try. Family ties stretched across an ocean where they formerly strained to stretch across a province.

Montreal, 1980

The New World in which we are living is an ever-changing society; thus, if we do not organize and reorganize, and adapt to new conditions, we will indeed find ourselves behind time. We must be careful, however, not to become obsessed by the idea of organization lest we organize for organization's sake. Organizing is not an end in itself; it is a means to an end.

Commencement Address,
St Vladimir's Seminary, 1981

In America we are always organizing, but people who organize are in constant danger of creating small kingdoms

105

for themselves. It is extremely difficult to take initiatives and develop new plans without claiming them as something that is yours. For example, how often do we hear priests saying, "I built this church and that hall, I established this mission and that parish." I, I, I, . . . as if God has nothing to do with our activities and daily lives. Our Lord said: "When you have done all that is commanded you, say, we are unworthy servants; we have only done what was our duty" (Luke 17:10).

Commencement Address,
St Vladimir's Seminary, 1981

The day Elias IV died was one of the saddest days of my life. June 21st, early in the morning, I went to the dining room to eat breakfast. The deacon was waiting for me sorrowful and with much anguish. I told him that I spent a very restless night and I even heard the phone ring around four o'clock in the morning. The deacon looked at me with tearful eyes and did not utter a word. When I finished breakfast, the deacon with a shaky voice, said: "The phone which you heard this morning was from Damascus. The Patriarch is dead." We looked at each other and with much grief burst into tears.

"On the Death of Patriarch Elias IV," 1979

Elias IV was born in the heights of the Lebanese mountains and although he left the village very young, the village never left him. His spontaneity and simplicity reflected this reality. He combined in his personality the gentleness of a soft midnight summer breeze and the explosiveness of a man who was impatient with everything. He was in this world but not of it. He was born poor, lived like a hermit and died like a meteor. His childhood impressions from the village never left him, hence his individualism, impatience with bureaucracies and all kinds of organizational structures. Elias

IV was a sensitive and intense poet; such sensitivity and intensity were always demonstrated in his prophetic words, penetrating eyes and constant hand gestures.

"On the Death of Patriarch Elias IV," 1979

Elias IV now belongs to history. He will always live in the conscience of the Church. His penetrating eyes are closed. His bright face is dust. His ever moving hands are still and his restless heart is finally at rest. Elias IV is no more, but our consolation lies in the fact that he was born on the peak, he lived on the peak and like an eagle, and he died on the peak.

"On the Death of Patriarch Elias IV," 1979

Three days after the Patriarch died, a little boy called me at the Archdiocese and said, "Is it true that the Holy Man died?" I said: "Yes, he did." The boy paused for a while and then said, "Good-bye," and that was the end of our conversation.

"On the Death of Patriarch Elias IV," 1979

The last Ecumenical Council was convened in 787 AD. This means that almost 1200 years have elapsed since the last Ecumenical Council which dealt mainly with the problem of iconoclasm. Many religious, moral, political and socio-economic events have taken place since 787 and deeply affected the life of the Church. One might ask: Why did the Church not meet since 787 to respond courageously and effectively to these challenges? Has the Church lost that dynamism and responsiveness which distinguished her life during the first ten centuries? There is no doubt that the Church has experienced very difficult times since the last Ecumenical Council. However, this does not excuse the stagnation which has marked her life for the past 1190 years. It is indeed strange that while we are active in the ecumenical movement attending World Council of Churches meetings in America, Europe, Asia, and Africa, we have no significant inter-Orthodox activities on either the national or international levels.

"Anticipating: On the Future of the Church in America," 1977

We will be forever indebted to our fathers and forefathers who have planted and nurtured the seeds of Orthodoxy in America, but our Mother Churches must realize once and for all that we are no longer a church of immigrants.

"Anticipating: On the Future of the Church in America," 1977

After the Arab-Israeli War of June 1967, I became involved in a humanitarian campaign to help alleviate some of the suffering of the Arab Refugees. January 5, 1968, I went to Washington, D.C. to meet with the Arab Ambassadors at the Lebanese Embassy in order to exchange views on the Middle Eastern crisis, and to offer my help to formulate a public relations program. This, I hoped, would give the American people the objective story on the Middle East, and help improve the Arab image in North America which was distorted by the news media and a most vicious political propaganda. I was shocked beyond measure when one of the Arab ambassadors whose country is floating on a sea of oil said to me, "You have a fine program, Your Eminence, start the work and we will help you." Needless to say that my conference with Their Excellencies ended in utter disappointment and despair. I could not understand what these ambassadors were doing in this country, which has been playing many roles in all Middle Eastern events since the end of the Second World War. That afternoon I suffered a heart attack.

"Personal Reflections," 1972

I grew up in a country where the bishop is the master and others are slaves. I grew up in a country where the bishop is untouchable, always frowning, always living in an ivory tower above the people, and especially, above the lower rank of the clergy. When I first met Metropolitan Antony, I felt completely at ease with him. I said to myself, "Thank God, at last, I met a bishop who celebrates life, who smiles, jokes, laughs, tells funny stories, weeps, works hard, and above all cares for ordinary people."

"On the Death of Metropolitan Antony," 1970

I am an Arab by birth, an American by choice; both realities weigh very heavily on my conscience. I represent neither the Arab governments nor the American administration. To me, this is an advantage. I am, first of all, a Christian and as such, I am free, free enough to represent, as an American, a defeated and a humiliated Arab generation.

Boston, 1982

The time has come to depart from empty rhetoric and meaningless slogans and cling to the truth. Christ said: "You shall know the truth and the truth shall make you free." I have already spent half of my life in the old country and the other half in my new country. Thus, I have experienced the eternal tension of the immigrant. Millions of us from the

Arabian Gulf to the Atlantic Ocean dreamt Arab dreams and saw visions; dreams of a united and strong Arab world, and visions of a just and liberated Arab society from without and from within. The sad events which have taken place in the Middle East during the past thirty-four years have shattered our dreams and destroyed our visions.

Boston, 1982

However, we cannot place all the blame for the Arab tragedy on American foreign policy alone. The late President Sadat used to say, "America holds ninety-nine per cent of the cards." I disagree with him and say, "The Arabs hold one hundred per cent of the cards." The question is: Can they play the game together? Unfortunately, the past thirty-four years have proved otherwise. There was a time in history when the Arabs were the leading world power, having excelled in all fields of endeavor: science, medicine, commerce, poetry, architecture and philosophy; but since the disintegration of the Arab empire, the Arabs have been living on the margin of history. Perhaps the past thirty-four years have been the darkest chapter in the entirety of Arab history. Arnold Toynbee, the British historian, described history as "a challenge and a response." The Arab response to the Zionist challenge has been most disappointing, despite their tremendous strategic, economic and human resources.

Boston, 1982

During our Bicentennial Year, 1976, the New England poet, Archibald MacLeish wrote: "We are as great as our belief in human liberty—no greater. And our belief in human liberty is only ours when it is larger than ourselves."

After the First World War, President Woodrow Wilson insisted that every international question should be settled "upon the basis of the free acceptance of that settlement by the people immediately concerned." Surely this principle was not applied to the Palestine and the people of the Middle East.

Boston, 1982

On June 6, 1982, the State of Israel lanuched a massive attack by land, sea and air against the Republic of Lebanon.

The fall and destruction of Tyre, Sidon, West Beirut and many other Lebanese villages and towns is reminiscent of the fall of the city of Jericho recorded in the Old Testament: "So the people shouted, and the trumpets were blown. As soon as the people heard the sound of the trumpets, the people raised a great shout, and the wall fell down flat, so that the people went up into the city, every man straight before him, and they took the city. Then they utterly destroyed all in the city, both men and women, young and old, oxen, sheep and asses, with the edge of the sword." (Joshua 6:20-21). Thousands of Lebanese citizens and Palestinian civilians are still detained by Israeli military authorities without any justification; and hundreds, according to eye-witness accounts, were beaten to death in flagrant violation of the principles of the Geneva Convention. This genocidal killing of men, women and children, coupled with mass destruction of Lebanese property, is an unprecedented act in a so-called civilzed world.

"Justice," 1982

According to the International Red Cross and the Lebanese Government, as of July 6, 1982, 10,000 Lebanese and Palestinians were killed; 20,000 were injured and maimed and 650,000 were made homeless. A western Ambassador, having returned from South Lebanon, and having seen the dimension of the tragedy remarked sadly, "I ask what has happened to those Jews who were filled with spirit and light, who gave us hope and inspiration, have they all gone? I came back from my trip to the south, and I am sick, sick at heart, sick to death."

"Justice," 1982

For many years the people of this Archdiocese have maintained that there will never be peace in the Middle East without a just solution to the problem of the Palestinian people. Dispersing the Palestinians into the Arab World will certainly not solve the problem. Only if and when the Palestinians establish their own state in their own homeland will the problem be solved.

"Justice," 1982

Israel and the Palestine Liberation Organization can win the battle of peace if they recognize each other and talk to each other. Peace can be won by negotiation rather than military confrontation. The Jewish people, who have suffered much throughout history, should have a sense of history and stop inflicting their past suffering on the Palestinian people. Peace can be won in the Middle East through justice, not cluster bombs.

"Justice," 1982

It is most unfortunate that we do not have a coherent and well-defined policy in the Middle East, based on justice for all and our own interests in that vital part of the world.

We have had presidents who have spoken about "Palestinian self-rule and the 'legitimate rights' of the Palestinian people." But the problems of the Middle East cannot be solved without self-determination for the Palestinians, and ultimately, the establishment of their own state on their own land, which they had inhabited since time immemorial.

Boston, 1982

Khali Hawi was one of the most brilliant poets of the Arab world. When the Israelis were savagely bombarding West Beirut without any resistance whatsoever from the Arab countries, Hawi committed suicide. He gave us a hint of his intensity when in one of his poems entitled, "The Bridge," Khali wrote: "When will we rise, become strong and build our new free home with our own hands? They will go and you will remain empty-handed, crucified, lonely, in the snowy nights, while the horizon is ashes of fire and bread is dust."

Boston, 1982

Anyone who examines our American policy *vis-a-vis* the Arab World cannot but ask these questions: What happened to the principles of the American Revolution? What happened to the precepts of that great Jeffersonian democracy which is unique in the history of mankind? Thomas Jefferson, the author of the American Declaration of Independence, a few days before his death, wrote to the citizens of Washington: "May it be to the whole world, what I believe it will be: to some parts sooner, to others later, but finally to all, the signal of arousing men to burst the chains. The mass of mankind has not been born with saddles on their backs for a favored few." These words from Thomas Jefferson indicate beyond doubt that freedom and equality among men has a global dimension.

Boston, 1982

Most of the early pioneers have died; however, the legacy which they left will never die. None of us can forget, however, that although they are spiritually rooted in Jerusalem, Tyre, Sidon, Beirut, Damascus and Antioch, their loyalty is first and foremost to America.

Montreal, 1980

About a century ago, hundreds of thousands of Syrian and Lebanese people, driven by the horror of tyranny, social injustice, oppression, hunger and despair, heard the voice which Abraham had heard, "Get thee out of thy country . . . unto a land that I will show thee." Thus from the Near East, mainly Lebanon, Syria and Palestine, wave after wave of immigrants have reached these blessed shores of America, their new home . . . They brought with them the spirituality of Peter, Paul, Ignatius of Antioch, and a cloud of witnesses of saints and martyrs who have willingly sacrificed their lives so that we may live. We celebrate the courage of those individuals who came to the New World and succeeded despite all difficulties and hardships.

Montreal, 1980

To my complete surprise, in 1966 I received the majority vote of the clergy and laity of our Archdiocese to be their new Metropolitan. But while the wishes of our Archdiocese were made crystal clear on this continent, there was on another continent a great measure of Synodical confusion, intrigues, conspiracies, and uncertainties. Dismayed and frustrated by the inaction of the Mother Church, our clergy and laity were most determined to preserve the sacred unity of our Archdiocese at all costs. Messages and messengers were sent to Antioch warning the Synod not to play with fire. Some of my friends during this period urged me to make a trip to the old country and meet informally with the Synod, but I refused to make the trip for the sake of my dignity and personal integrity.

Finally, on the Eve of the great Feast of the Transfiguration, the Holy Synod of Antioch honored the wishes of our Archdiocese and elected me to succeed Metropolitan Antony in this holy ministry. Thus on August 14, 1966, I was elevated to the rank of the episcopate amongst family members, relatives, friends, and hundreds of curious people who came to St Elias Monastery to catch a glimpse of the controversial American archbishop. Needless to say, that August 14 was one of the most emotional days of my life. After the consecration I had to rush back to San Francisco via the Far East in order to preside over the Annual Convention of the Archdiocese. When I reached San Francisco, I was emotionally drained and physically exhausted and until now, I do not know how I survived that convention. From San Francisco I returned to Lebanon to participate in the meeting of the Holy Synod which was still in session. The meetings of the Holy Synod lacked order, discipline, seriousness and future vision, to such a degree, that after I left the meeting very disappointed, I went to my room and wept bitterly.

"The Election and First Events," 1970

I am indeed delighted that our Orthodox situation in America will be discussed at the "Great Synod," which I pray will convene. I wonder, however, how much the venerable hierarchs of the Church in the Old World really know about our Orthodox situation in America. It is, therefore, our sacred responsibility to provide our Orthodox brethren across the ocean with a true and clear picture about our successes and failures, especially during the current century.

"Anticipating: On the Future
of the Church in America," 1977

Our brethren in the Old World must realize that Orthodoxy on this continent is no longer a child. In his book, *The Individual and His Orthodox Church*, Father Nicon Patrinacos states: "The American Orthodox of today, having come of age as regards his personal religious experience and that of the group within which he moves, seeks a more definite and convincing articulation of his faith and a way of practicing it, to which he could fully subscribe without hesitation or reservation, and without fear of being severed on account of it from his American environment." He is correct.

"Anticipating: On the Future of the Church in America," 1977

It is indeed astonishing that we have not had an Ecumenical Council since 787 A.D. despite the many changes which the Church has encountered during the past one thousand, one hundred ninety-seven years. I shall mention but a few of these global events which affected the life of the Church directly or indirectly since the last Ecumenical Council:

The 1054 Schism between East and West.
The Fall of Constantinople.
The European Renaissance with all its implications.
The Protestant Reformation.
The Discovery of the New World.
The French Revolution.
The Industrial Revolution.
The Communist Revolution and its impact on the Orthodox Church.
The First and Second World Wars.
Dawning of the Nuclear Age.
The exploration of space and all the scientific and technological discoveries which baffle the mind.

Despite all these significant events which have deeply touched our lives, we Orthodox are still debating whether or not we should convene the Eighth Ecumenical Council.

Worcester, 1984

In 1967, after the Arab defeat at the hands of the Israelis, the news media and the news commentators made a mockery of the Arab nations. Even the weathermen laughed and made sarcastic remarks against the Arabs. Those of us who have pride in our heritage and national background were subjected, especially in New York City, to the most pathetic and humiliating experience. Subsequent to the June War, I started a national campaign to raise money for the Arab refugees—a campaign which took me to many cities all over the United States and Canada.

I believe that the aforementioned emotional events and many others have contributed directly and indirectly to my heart collapse in Washington, D.C. in January 1968.

"Personal Reflections," 1972

We consider ourselves Americans and we are proud of it, except when we go to church. We suddenly become Greeks, Russians, Arabs, Albanians and so forth.

Worcester, 1984

We must make a firm decision that we are here in America to stay. I say this because some of us, clergy and laity, at least psychologically, are still in the old country. Orthodoxy on this continent will remain insignificant and ineffective as long as we continue to live in our ethnic ghettos. Consequently, if we do not express our inner unity in concrete, external action, we will continue this insignificant presence for many years to come.

"On Contemporary Iconoclasm," Pittsburgh, 1976

In the autumn of 1966, I returned from Lebanon to the United States to begin my work in the Archdiocese. I will never forget that horrible October day when I entered the

Archdiocese home in Bay Ridge alone. Tired from traveling and the events of the past months, I was desperately in need of help. There was the Archbishop of New York and all North America in an old house without a cook, a secretary, a priest or even a custodian which most parishes provide for their priests. The Archdiocese of New York and all North America was one man: Metropolitan Antony Bashir, and when he died there was no organization.

"The Year of Difficulties and Loneliness," 1970

Since my early youth I have always been proud of my people, their glorious history and tremendous contribution to world civilization. I believe that their heroic struggle to establish themselves in North America is one of the greatest human dramas ever written. Our people lack neither intelligence nor ambition. However, since the disintegration of the Arab Empire they have been plagued by dissension and disunity. And despite their unique strategic place on the global map and the tremendous natural resources which they possess, they have never been able to use all these advantages to influence world opinion in their fight for an honorable and just peace in the Middle East.

"Personal Reflections," 1972

Subsequent to the Pan-Orthodox consultations in Switzerland, in which thirteen patriarchates and churches were represented, a proposed agenda of ten points was approved for the "Great Synod." I was not much impressed with the agenda after 1190 ylears of expectation; some of its topics are outdated and irrelevant.

"Anticipating: On the Future of the Church in America," 1977

I am dissatisfied because the Holy Synod of Antioch is still engaged in vain talk and fruitless debate and has lost its sense of history and destiny. When sacred duty called us to cross the ocean last April to Lebanon to attend the meetings of the Holy Synod, we did it gladly because of our devotion to the Mother Church. But, my friends, "we have labored all night long to no avail." After twenty-five days of meetings we accomplished nothing except the reading of the Minutes of the last Synod Meeting. We experienced much distress and frustration, and came back convinced beyond the shadow of a doubt that we must work hard for a united Orthodoxy in America for our own sake and for the sake of the Mother Churches. We shall continue to support the See of Antioch both spiritually and financially, but we are not willing to waste time anymore on nothingness. The only joy which we had during our trip was derived from our visit with the young seminarians at the Balamand School. The new Theological Academy which we are building there is almost completed, but we have no idea how this academy is going to be staffed or operated financially. Only the Almighty God knows.

In Northern Lebanon, a beautiful hill covered with pine trees overlooking the blue Mediterranean from the West, and gazing at the peaks of the cedars from the East, there stands the new Academy as a living witness of your continued support to the Mother Church. Although we have received little from Antioch for giving much to Antioch, we shall continue to support this school and the Patriarchate regardless of future developments. It is your nature to give, sacrifice, work and love. Dostoevsky said:

If you love everything, you will perceive the Divine Mystery in things. Once you perceive it, you will begin to comprehend it better every day. And you will come at last to love the whole world, with an all-embracing love.

In Arabic we say, "An idle mind is a playground for the devil."

Los Angeles, 1972

My visit to Russia was one of the most significant experiences of my entire life. You may hear stories or read books about the Church in Russia, but unless you go there and experience for yourself the spiritual depth of the Russian people, your knowledge of the Russian spirituality remains purely academic. Despite the limited freedom which the Church enjoys under an atheistic government, it is not unusual in Russia to celebrate Vespers and Divine Liturgies with five, ten or twenty-five thousand faithful. The Russians have no pews in their churches, yet they stand and pray with eyes fixed on heaven, pouring out their hearts with soft tears before the Almighty God. While in Russia, we visited some of the most beautiful churches in the world, in Moscow, Leningrad and Zagorsk. Every icon in Russia is a window to heaven, and every church in Russia is a little piece of heaven. If you look at Moscow or Leningrad from the air, you see nothing but church cupolas piercing the sky. At every turn of the road there is a church; a constant reminder that Christ, and not Marx, is the Lord of history. It is one of the contradictions of life that the most spiritual people on earth have to live under the most Godless and materialistic system.

"On His Visit to Russia," Washington, D.C. 1977

I told my hosts, almost on every occasion, that Russian history without the Church is meaningless, and that the land which gave the world spiritual and intellectual giants such as Seraphim of Sorov, Nil of Sora, Tolstoy, Dostoevsky, Tschiakovsky, Rachmaninov, Nicholas Berdyaev, George Florovsky and Aleksandr Solzhenitsyn, will never be crucified forever. Beyond Calvary there is the empty tomb. On this hope the

Russian people live and wait for the heavy stone to be rolled away from the door of the sepulchre.

"On His Visit to Russia," Washington, D.C. 1977

(1976)   The war in Lebanon is now in its sixteenth month. We are very much concerned with this tragedy because many of us have families and relatives there. Moreover, whether we are of Arab descent or not, our spiritual roots lie deeply in that beautiful soil which has been stained by the blood of innocent men, women and children. Words are inadequate to describe to you the depth of this tragedy. You ask about friends and relatives in Lebanon and these are some of the answers which you receive:

This one was killed by a rocket while at home.
This one was killed by a sniper's bullet while going
to buy bread for his children.
That family was burned to death by fire.

"On the War in Lebanon," San Francisco, 1976

On April 15th, we visited the President of the United States and urged him to use his good offices to bring this war to an end. The President had already dispatched Dean Brown to Lebanon to mediate the crisis. His efforts were for naught. The President seemed genuinely concerned with Lebanon and its reconstruction, but unfortunately, the war persists.

Who is to blame for this tragedy? There is no simple answer to this question. However, I believe that the leaders of the Lebanese right and the leaders of the Lebanese left are to be blamed. I believe that the Palestinians are also to be blamed, for instead of dedicating all their efforts and energy to liberate their land, they are dying in Lebanon for nothing.

But above all, I believe that the Arab countries who have demonstrated their complete impotence *vis-a-vis* this tragedy, are to be blamed. It is time that the Arabs should stop blaming others for their tragedies and liberate themselves from their childish bickering and stupid contradictions.

"On the War in Lebanon," San Francisco, 1976

Your Beatitude, around the end of the last century, thousands of Antiochian faithful were forced to leave their motherland, seeking freedom and social justice in the New World. Unfortunately, some of them died in North Africa and Europe and never made it here. Fortunately, however, many of them did reach Ellis Island in the New York harbor. They had no money, no skills and did not speak the language. The lucky ones had an address of a friend somewhere in this land. Many of them had to sleep in the streets before they found a humble shelter. They purchased some light merchandise and peddled it from city to city, town to town and state to state. The first thing they did was to establish a church in some house, in order to preserve their spiritual heritage. It is important to note here that many of our parishes were established by lay people before our bishops and priests arrived to this continent. Hence, the strong lay orientation of our Church in North America. Our people were lucky if a priest visited them once a year to marry them, baptize their children and pray for their dead.

These simple, early pioneers were the true heroes of Orthodoxy in this New World. Besides their stubborn clinging to the Holy Orthodox Faith, they proved to be good citizens of their new, adopted country. They were determined to educate their children and instill in them their traditions and values such as hard work, honesty and decency.

Your Beatitude, the early immigrants have laid the foundation of this Archdiocese. Today, almost one hundred years later, if we reflect on the history of our Archdiocese, we may distinguish three main eras: the era of immigration which was the most difficult, the era of organization and the era of spiritual maturation.

Your Beatitude, these humble achievements and many others which were realized, especially during the past nineteen years, are not the fruit of my efforts alone. They are the result of perfect cooperation between the bishop, the clergy and the laity. We in this Archdiocese cherish this sound Orthodox principle and whenever this principle is violated, the whole life of the Church is violated.

"Addressing Patriarch Ignatius," Boston, 1985

During the Apostolic Era, Antioch was the main center of missionary activities. There was a time when the See of Antioch encompassed the whole East. Antioch was glorified by the martyrdom of its third bishop, St Ignatius of Antioch, by the melodies of Romanos of Homs, by the poetry of St Ephraim the Syrian, by the eloquence of St John Chrysostom and by the genius of St John of Damascus. This is to mention but a few of the great Antiochian saints. I am not trying to be parochial by stating these facts. I do not know of anyone who has focused on the catholicity of the Church more than the Antiochian Fathers. In a lecture which His Beatitude, Patriarch Ignatius, delivered two years ago at the Sorbonne University in Paris, he said: "The Christianity of the Church of Antioch, just as Christ Himself, belongs neither to the East nor to the West." During the early Christian period, Antioch developed its own school of architecture, monasticism, and theology. What we call today, the incarnational school of theology, is deeply rooted in the Antiochian Fathers.

Patriarch Ignatius IV represents much glory and yet much suffering. As a matter of fact, the land of Antioch is still drenched by the blood of confessors and martyrs. I shall briefly mention some of the calamities which Antioch suffered throughout history. From Calvary to the Edict of Milan, Antioch has suffered the most barbarous and longest holocaust under the pagan Roman empire. This was followed by the Persian invasion and the internal heresies which have torn Antioch asunder, the Muslim conquest of the Near East, the Crusades, the Ottoman Turks, the western missionaries, the Melkite schism and last, but not least, international Zionism. It is a miracle, indeed, that Antioch is still alive. Perhaps it is the destiny of Antioch to wash away the sins of the world with her tears and blood.

"Addressing Patriarch Ignatius," Boston, 1985

Your Beatitude and most beloved Father,

Your visit to this Archdiocese has been an explosion of love. During the past two and a half months, you have traveled to every region of this Archdiocese and touched every heart. You have seen us in our strength and in our weakness. Rest assured, Your Beatitude, that the beautiful memories of your visit will linger in our minds for many, many years to come and wherever you go, you will always be surrounded by our love and prayers.

Our fervent supplication shall always be:

Among the first be mindful, O Lord, of our Father, Patriarch Ignatius, whom do thou grant unto the Holy Church in peace, safety, honor, health and length of days and faithfully proclaiming the Word of Thy truth.

"Addressing Patriarch Ignatius," Boston, 1985

We are tired of division. We want Orthodoxy to unite and face the challenges of our time, not only in North America, but all over the world. We of the Antiochian Archdiocese know well the agony of division. We have suffered this agony for sixty years; then in a bright moment of our history, our people were reunited in the strongest Archdiocese in the Patriarchate of Antioch and, perhaps, in the entire

Orthodox world. I want you to be vigilant, watchful, strong and guard this unity with your mighty arms. The other day, I heard a rumor to this effect: "after the death of Metropolitan Philip, this Archdiocese will be divided." Do you want history to repeat itself? Do you want brothers to fight brothers, cousins to fight cousins and neighbors to fight neighbors? We have already gone through our long, dark night. Do you want to be divided again? Even if the angels come and tell you "division is good for you," do not believe them.

Los Angeles, 1981

Surely, love transcends all barriers. Patriarch Elias IV represents two thousand years of spirituality. He comes to us as the successor of Saints Peter and Paul, St Ignatius of Antioch, St John Chrysostom, St John of Damascus and a "cloud of witnesses" of martyrs and ascetics. I have read lately that after the famous TV series, "Roots," many Americans have been trying to rediscover their ancestral and cultural origins. In our case, we do not have to try hard. Our spiritual roots are deeply planted in Bethlehem, Nazareth, Galilee, Jerusalem, Beirut, Damascus and Antioch.

Patriarch Elias IV represents all this glory, yet he represents much suffering. History has not been very kind to us. From Ignatius to Elias IV, the history of Antioch has been written in blood. Antioch knows very well the meaning of martyrdom, persecution, oppression, controversy and even heresy. Strange is the Antiochian mind! Many times while trying to focus on the transcendent God, it went beyond its limits and fell into heresy. Yes, we have suffered much throughout history, from so-called Christians and non-Christians alike.

Washington, D.C., 1977

Your Beatitude and beloved Father, when you accepted

our invitation to visit this North American continent, we rejoiced and decided to initiate a project in order to express to you our thanks and gratitude. Sixteen years ago while returning from a frustrating trip to the Holy Synod of Antioch, the late Metropolitan Antony said to me, "The only way to create a spiritual renaissance in the Patriarchate of Antioch is to build a theological Academy for the entire Middle East." I could not agree with him more, because the Patriarchates of Jerusalem, Alexandria and even Constantinople all are without theological academies. Unfortunately, Metropolitan Antony died in February 1966, before the realization of his dream. This Archdiocese, with its Board of Trustees and all its faithful, was determined to accomplish this task without any hesitation or delay. We expended the money, we broke ground for the new school in August 1966, and in 1971, Patriarch Elias IV dedicated this beautiful academy which will always stand as an expression of our love for our Mother Church.

Washington, D.C., 1977

Our hope is that out of all the tears, sorrows, destruction, panic, starvation, displacement and calamities of the past difficult years, a new Lebanon be born where there would be place neither for exploitation nor for compromising against the nation or the individual citizen. It seems to me, after all these difficulties that poured over that country, that the foundations upon which modern Lebanon had been built were not correct.

"On the Lebanese Conflict," 1986

Is it imaginable that in the modern political arena someone may attain a certain position which would be forbidden to another on the mere basis of religious affiliation? Is this not demeaning the human value of the individual and refusing him his civil rights? If we are indeed citizens equal in rights and responsibilities, then it is the right of each to pursue any office disregarding his religious or political affiliation. And any nation that does not guarantee its citizens such elementary human rights is bound to disappear. Thus, the correct way to building the new Lebanon is to first get rid of political confessionalism and the prepare the Lebanese society to accept full laicization—in its political, not philosophical understanding—that would unite the Lebanese society into a unified entity and would guarantee the freedom of thought and belief even to the non-believers.

"On the Lebanese Conflict," 1986

Metropolitan Philip's Consecration Speech

August 14, 1966

(Given at St Elias Monastery in Dhour Shweir, Lebanon)

Your Beatitude, Brother Members of the Holy Synod and Faithful Orthodox:

With much longing, we left the New World for this good land which was blessed by the footsteps of Jesus of Nazareth. We bring to you greetings, love and sincere obedience from your spiritual children in the United States and Canada. It is indeed a great honor for me, your Beatitude and beloved brothers, to receive the grace of the Holy Episcopate through the laying on of your blessed hands which are laboring tirelessly to revive the glory of Antioch which gave Christianity thousands of saints, confessors and martyrs.

On the 16th and 17th of March 1966, the clergy and laity of the Archdiocese of New York and all North America overwhelmingly nominated me to be their future shepherd. Before the nomination, however, I told the assembled clergy and laity, openly and publicly, that I am not worthy of this Divine Grace, although it "heals the sick and completest that which is wanting," and that we human beings are powerless without the help and mercy of God. Yet, the pious clergy and faithful laity proceeded with my nomination, despite my weakness and sins which are more numerous than the sand of the seas.

When Metropolitan Antony Bashir, of thrice-blessed memory, ordained me to the priesthood in 1959 to serve St

129

George Parish of Cleveland, Ohio, I said in my ordination speech, the following: "In 1948, I left the Balamand Seminary and its quiet life and returned to society and its problems. Thus, an era of doubt, anxiety and rebelliousness began in my life. During this period, I lost some of my faith in the Church because I could not differentiate the Church as a human institution subject to sins and tribulations, and the Church as a divine institution for which Christ died and was resurrected from the dead, 'that He might present her to Himself in splendor, without spot or wrinkle or any such thing, that she might be holy and without blemish' (Eph 5:27). Tormented by doubt, despair and confusion, I found refuge in some secular religions, but it was not long before God visited me and said, 'Rise and stand upon your feet, for I have appeared to you for this purpose, to appoint you to serve and bear witness to the things in which you have seen me and to those in which I will appear to you' (Acts 26:16). Thus, I returned to Christ to find in Him the right answer, not only to my personal problems, but also to the problems of humankind and history."

When the Church was as pure as the light which shone on Tabor, the early Christians publicly confessed their sins before the congregation because the sins which we commit are not against God only, but also against the community. At my priestly ordination, I have confessed my sins openly, and today I confess again before God and this congregation that I have sinned more than the publican and the prodigal son, like Paul and Augustine. From the depth of my heart, I cry like David, "Have mercy on me, O God, according to Thy steadfast love, according to Thine abundant mercy. Blot out my transgression. Wash me thoroughly from my iniquity and cleanse me from my sins. For I know my transgression, and my sin is ever before me. Against Thee only have I sinned and done evil in Thy sight so that Thou are justified in thy sentence and blameless in Thy judgment. Behold I was brought forth in iniquity and in sin did my mother conceive me" (Psalm 51).

All of us in the Church of Antioch, clergy and laity alike, must lament our transgressions like David, weep like the adulterous woman, humble ourselves like the publican, confess like the thief on the cross and repent like the prodigal son; that repentance which was described by St Isaac the Syrian as, "the trembling of the soul at the gates of paradise." My prayer has been, still is and will always be the prayer of the Church which knocks on the door of repentance with sinful hands.

I thank God, however, that Pharisaism never found a way to my heart, and I have never tried to judge anyone. Only He who knows "the secrets of the heart" will judge each one of us according to his or her deeds.

Your Beatitude, brother and sisters:

In the Epistle to the Hebrews, it is said: "For every high priest chosen from among men is appointed to act on behalf of men in relation to God, to offer gifts and sacrifices for sins" (Heb 5:1). The episcopate, therefore, is not a worldly, vain glory. The episcopate is first and foremost sacrifice, service and love. The episcopate is the continuation of the eternal priesthood of Christ in time and space. Thus, the bishop's authority is neither autocratic, nor arbitrary, nor absolute; it is an authority based on love and service, for "if anyone would be first, he must be last of all and servant of all" (Mark 9:35). Armed with such lofty Christian principles, we launch into our pastoral work in the Archdiocese of New York and North America, which is an integral part of the Holy See of Antioch, the See of Peter, Paul and Theodosius IV. All our means in North America are at your disposal, and tomorrow we shall be delighted indeed to accompany His Beatitude to the holy hills of Balamand to lay the cornerstone of the theological academy which our predecessor, Metropolitan Antony, had pledged to erect to help the Mother Church.

It is impossible for Antioch to become the bride of Christ and a hymn of praise to Him without a theological institute to breathe life in this Orthodox East where the storms of civil strife, divisiveness, doubt and despair are blowing from all directions. It is impossible for Antioch to recapture its past glory unless it elevates itself from the stagnant swamps of cheap politics to the esplanades of truth, goodness and beauty. We never wanted Antioch to be Eastern or Western in the political sense. We always wanted Antioch an Orthodox Christian Church, free, independent, committed to the love of God and neighbor, obedient to the Patriarch, the Holy Synod and canons of ecumenical and local councils; such canons which were written by the blood of martyrs in order to enlighten and guide those who are tempted to rebel against the authority of the Church.

Your Beatitude,

We shall never bargain on the truth which liberated us from the bondage of sin. Did the Holy Fathers betray the Church when they were forced to celebrate the Eucharist in the caves and catacombs? Did the martyrs of the twentieth century Church bargain on the truth when thousands of them went to prisons and gallows in atheistic countries? Anyone who bargains with falsehood and sells his soul to the devil will have to answer God on the Day of Judgment.

We promise Your Beatitude that we shall work with you and our venerable brothers to encourage and promote the youth movements here and in North America, for the faithful youth are the heartbeat of the Church. We assure Your Beatitude and our beloved brothers that our doors and hearts will always be open to you, and we hope that you will bless us with your visits from time to time in order to witness the discipline, faith and progress which the Archdiocese of New York and all North America has attained.

We realize that our road is long and difficult, covered with stones and thorns, full of hissing reptiles and howling wolves. But He who has crushed the head of the serpent and calmed the sea will raise us up when we stumble and lead us to the right path.

(translated from the Arabic)

Paschal Meditation
1971

By Metropolitan Philip

Lord, I am talking to you between airports, between flights, in the midst of rushing crowds and noisy engines. Please forgive me if my words are vain and empty. The last time I talked to you, you were in a lonely manger. As I stared at you, I saw the wounds in your tiny hands, the spear in your tender side and the crown of thorns on your bleeding head.

Lord, Every time I gaze at your Crucifix I tremble with fear and ask myself, "Why did you love me so much?" I should be hanging there in your stead. I rebelled against you in paradise. I murdered my brother in the field. I betrayed you in Gethsemane. And when they crucified you I was the leader of the gang.

Lord, Why do you love me so much? I do not deserve one drop of your sweat, one drop of your tears, and one drop of your blood. Why did you wash my filthy feet? Why did you share your body and blood with my unworthy lips?

Lord, Why did you weep over my Jerusalem? The streets of the city which you loved are still stained with your innocent blood and the tears of your little friends in Jerusalem have become rivers of suffering and agony. Your little friends in your land, Lord, are drinking their Mother's tears and eating their Mother's flesh but no one cares.

Lord, You called me "friend," but at the night of trial I cursed, I swore, and I said, "I know not that man." Instead of water I gave you vinegar, and when that heavy cross was crushing your shoulders I did not lift a finger to help you.

Lord, You had reached the abyss of agony and despair when you cried with a mighty voice, "My God, my God, why hast thou forsaken me?" This was your last cry in this world before you gave up the spirit, and it fell on deaf ears. After that you died. "And there was darkness all over the land."

Lord, Beyond the innocence of Bethlehem, the tears of Gethsemane, and the agony of Calvary, there is the joy of the new wine, the brightness of the new dawn, the hope of the new creation and the eternal reality of the empty tomb.
"O Death where is thy sting?"
"O Hell where is thy victory?"

Lord, Let the immortal light of your Pascha penetrate the thickness of our dark nights. Roll away the heavy stones from the doors of our sepulchers. Liberate us by your Divine Freedom. Wash away all our iniquities,
"O Lamb of God who takest away the sins of the world."